Exclusive Online Reso

As our valued reader, your purchase of this book includes access to exclusive online resources designed to enhance your learning experience. These resources can be downloaded from our website, www.vibrantpublishers.com, and are created to help you apply Java® concepts effectively.

Online resources for this book include the following:

1. Java codes used in the book
2. Additional coding tasks

Why are these online resources valuable:

- **Practical application:** The downloadable codes are provided for easy testing and use.
- **Enhanced learning experience:** The additional coding tasks will provide hands-on experience and help you apply the knowledge learned from the book in practical scenarios.

How to access your online resources:

1. **Visit the website:** Go to www.vibrantpublishers.com
2. **Find your book:** Navigate to the book's product page via the "Shop" menu or by searching for the book title in the search bar.
3. **Request the resources:** Scroll down to the "Request Sample Book/Online Resource" section.
4. **Enter your details:** Enter your preferred email ID and select "Online Resource" as the resource type. Lastly, select "user type" and submit the request.
5. **Check your inbox:** The resources will be delivered directly to your email.

Alternatively, for quick access: simply scan the QR code below to go directly to the product page and request the online resources by filling in the required details.

https://bit.ly/jv1-slm

Happy learning!

SELF-LEARNING MANAGEMENT SERIES

VIBRANT
PUBLISHERS

JAVA®
ESSENTIALS

VOLUME 1: PROGRAMMING FUNDAMENTALS

COVERS UPDATES UP TO JDK 23

Take your first steps into Java programming with
clear lessons, simple code, and hands-on learning

LAWRENCE DECAMORA
MICHELLE DECAMORA

JAVA® ESSENTIALS VOLUME 1: PROGRAMMING FUNDAMENTALS

First Edition

Published by Vibrant Publishers LLC, USA, www.vibrantpublishers.com

Paperback ISBN 13: 978-1-63651-502-1
Ebook ISBN 13: 978-1-63651-503-8
Hardback ISBN 13: 978-1-63651-504-5
Library of Congress Control Number: 2025939620

This publication is designed to provide accurate and authoritative information regarding the subject matter covered. The Author has made every effort in the preparation of this book to ensure the accuracy of the information. However, information in this book is sold without warranty, either expressed or implied. The Author or the Publisher will not be liable for any damages caused or alleged to be caused either directly or indirectly by this book.

All trademarks and registered trademarks mentioned in this publication are the property of their respective owners, including but not limited to Java and Oracle. These trademarks are used for editorial and educational purposes only, without intent to infringe upon any trademark rights. This publication is independent and has not been authorized, endorsed, or approved by any trademark owner.

All screenshots from Oracle products copyright © Oracle Corporation and/or its affiliates. Used with permission.

Screenshots from the NetBeans Integrated Development Environment (IDE) are reproduced under the terms of the Apache License, Version 2.0, and are used solely for educational and illustrative purposes.

Vibrant Publishers' books are available at special quantity discounts for sales promotions, or for use in corporate training programs. For more information, please write to bulkorders@vibrantpublishers.com

Please email feedback/corrections (technical, grammatical, or spelling) to spellerrors@vibrantpublishers.com

Vibrant publishes in a variety of print and electronic formats and by print-on-demand. Some material included with standard print versions of this book may not be included in e-books in print-on-demand. To access the complete catalog of Vibrant Publishers, visit www.vibrantpublishers.com

SELF-LEARNING MANAGEMENT SERIES

TITLE	PAPERBACK* ISBN

BUSINESS AND ENTREPRENEURSHIP

Title	ISBN
BUSINESS COMMUNICATION ESSENTIALS	9781636511634
BUSINESS ETHICS ESSENTIALS	9781636513324
BUSINESS LAW ESSENTIALS	9781636511702
BUSINESS PLAN ESSENTIALS	9781636511214
BUSINESS STRATEGY ESSENTIALS	9781949395778
ENTREPRENEURSHIP ESSENTIALS	9781636511603
INTERNATIONAL BUSINESS ESSENTIALS	9781636513294
PRINCIPLES OF MANAGEMENT ESSENTIALS	9781636511542

COMPUTER SCIENCE AND TECHNOLOGY

Title	ISBN
BLOCKCHAIN ESSENTIALS	9781636513003
CYBERSECURITY ESSENTIALS	9781636514888
MACHINE LEARNING ESSENTIALS	9781636513775
PYTHON ESSENTIALS	9781636512938

DATA SCIENCE FOR BUSINESS

Title	ISBN
BUSINESS ANALYTICS ESSENTIALS	9781636514154
BUSINESS INTELLIGENCE ESSENTIALS	9781636513362
DATA ANALYTICS ESSENTIALS	9781636511184

FINANCIAL LITERACY AND ECONOMICS

Title	ISBN
COST ACCOUNTING & MANAGEMENT ESSENTIALS	9781636511030
FINANCIAL ACCOUNTING ESSENTIALS	9781636510972
FINANCIAL MANAGEMENT ESSENTIALS	9781636511009
MACROECONOMICS ESSENTIALS	9781636511818
MICROECONOMICS ESSENTIALS	9781636511153
PERSONAL FINANCE ESSENTIALS	9781636511849
PRINCIPLES OF ECONOMICS ESSENTIALS	9781636512334

*Also available in Hardback & Ebook formats

SELF-LEARNING MANAGEMENT SERIES

TITLE	PAPERBACK* ISBN

HR, DIVERSITY, AND ORGANIZATIONAL SUCCESS

DIVERSITY, EQUITY, AND INCLUSION ESSENTIALS	9781636512976
DIVERSITY IN THE WORKPLACE ESSENTIALS	9781636511122
HR ANALYTICS ESSENTIALS	9781636510347
HUMAN RESOURCE MANAGEMENT ESSENTIALS	9781949395839
ORGANIZATIONAL BEHAVIOR ESSENTIALS	9781636512303
ORGANIZATIONAL DEVELOPMENT ESSENTIALS	9781636511481

LEADERSHIP AND PERSONAL DEVELOPMENT

DECISION MAKING ESSENTIALS	9781636510026
INCLUSIVE LEADERSHIP ESSENTIALS	9781636514765
INDIA'S ROAD TO TRANSFORMATION: WHY LEADERSHIP MATTERS	9781636512273
LEADERSHIP ESSENTIALS	9781636510316
TIME MANAGEMENT ESSENTIALS	9781636511665

MODERN MARKETING AND SALES

CONSUMER BEHAVIOR ESSENTIALS	9781636513263
DIGITAL MARKETING ESSENTIALS	9781949395747
MARKETING MANAGEMENT ESSENTIALS	9781636511788
MARKET RESEARCH ESSENTIALS	9781636513744
MODERN ADVERTISING ESSENTIALS	9781636514857
SALES MANAGEMENT ESSENTIALS	9781636510743
SERVICES MARKETING ESSENTIALS	9781636511733
SOCIAL MEDIA MARKETING ESSENTIALS	9781636512181

*Also available in Hardback & Ebook formats

SELF-LEARNING MANAGEMENT SERIES

TITLE	PAPERBACK* ISBN
OPERATIONS MANAGEMENT	
AGILE ESSENTIALS	9781636510057
OPERATIONS & SUPPLY CHAIN MANAGEMENT ESSENTIALS	9781949395242
PRODUCT MANAGEMENT ESSENTIALS	9781636514796
PROJECT MANAGEMENT ESSENTIALS	9781636510712
STAKEHOLDER ENGAGEMENT ESSENTIALS	9781636511511
CURRENT AFFAIRS	
DIGITAL SHOCK	9781636513805

*Also available in Hardback & Ebook formats

About the Authors

Lawrence G. Decamora III, Ph.D., is an accomplished computer science educator, author, and industry professional with extensive experience in software development and academia. Holding prestigious certifications including Sun Certified Java Programmer (SCJP) and Oracle Certified Professional Java Programmer (OCPJP), he has contributed significantly to the field of information technology.

Dr. Decamora has been a dedicated instructor in computer science, information systems, and information technology for over two decades. He has taught at renowned institutions such as the University of Santo Tomas, De La Salle-College of Saint Benilde, and Mapua Institute of Technology. His academic leadership includes serving as the Acting ITE Program Director and an Academic Head, mentoring countless students and aspiring IT professionals.

In the industry, Dr. Decamora has collaborated with leading organizations like Sun Microsystems Philippines, Phoenix One, and ActiveLearning Inc., providing Java training and software development solutions. His expertise spans Java programming, enterprise applications, and web technologies.

Beyond teaching, Dr. Decamora is a sought-after speaker and trainer, having conducted seminars and workshops on Java programming, software engineering, and emerging technologies. His passion for knowledge sharing is evident in his commitment to empowering learners through practical insights and real-world applications.

This book is a testament to his dedication to making Java accessible to learners at all levels. Through clear explanations and hands-on examples, Dr. Decamora continues to inspire and guide the next generation of developers.

Michelle C. Decamora, MIT, is a dedicated educator and experienced IT professional with a passion for empowering students through knowledge and hands-on learning. With a Master's in Information Technology and extensive teaching experience, she has made significant contributions to the field of computer science education.

Michelle has served as an Information Technology Instructor at esteemed institutions, including CIIT College of Arts and Technology and De La Salle-College of Saint Benilde. Her commitment to academic excellence extends beyond the classroom, having previously held leadership roles such as Academic Supervisor and Head at Systems Technology Institute (STI), Malabon, where she supervised faculty, developed curricula, and ensured academic quality.

Michelle's expertise in database management, Java programming, and application development has equipped her with a comprehensive understanding of both theoretical and practical aspects of IT.

In addition to her teaching role, Michelle has attended numerous specialized training programs, including IBM DB2 Academic Training, AutoCAD with Color Rendering, and advanced Macromedia Flash application development. Her dedication to continuous learning has earned her recognition, including the IBM Certified Academic Associate credential in DB2 Database and Application Fundamentals.

As a co-author of this book, Michelle shares her wealth of knowledge and practical insights to guide learners in their journey into Java programming. Her collaborative approach to teaching and passion for fostering student growth make her an invaluable contributor to this educational resource.

What Experts Say About This Book!

Lawrence Decamora has crafted an exceptionally well-structured introduction to Java programming that stands out in the crowded field of programming textbooks. As an educator myself, I'm impressed by the book's thoughtful progression from fundamental concepts to practical application.

What makes this book particularly valuable is its "learning while practicing" philosophy. Rather than overwhelming beginners with abstract theory, Lawrence guides readers through hands-on experiences that build confidence incrementally. The integration of JShell for interactive learning is brilliant and reflects modern pedagogical best practices.

The book's comprehensive coverage—from JDK installation across multiple operating systems to essential programming concepts like control structures, arrays, and string manipulation—provides students with a solid foundation. Each chapter's careful construction, complete with exercises, quizzes, and coding tasks, ensures that concepts are not merely memorized but truly understood.

Lawrence's emphasis on real-world programming practices, including debugging techniques and coding conventions, prepares students for actual development work rather than just academic exercises. The clear writing style and logical progression make complex concepts accessible to beginners while maintaining the depth necessary for serious learning.

This volume effectively sets the stage for more advanced topics to be covered in Volume 2, making it an excellent choice for educational institutions and self-directed learners alike.

– David Smith, CEO,
Silicon Valley High School, Inc.

As someone who has seen Lawrence's teaching style up close, especially when we worked together on the on-demand Java course for LearningWhilePracticing, I'm not at all surprised by how clear, structured, and pedagogically strong this book is. That same clarity and hands-on mindset translate beautifully onto the page. The explanations are precise without being overwhelming, and the pacing feels just right. Concepts are introduced gradually, with each chapter building logically on the previous one. The inclusion of chapter summaries, quizzes, and coding tasks at the end of each section is a fantastic way to reinforce learning.

The structure is excellent. From installing the JDK all the way to understanding arrays, the content covers exactly what a beginner needs to gain confidence. It also goes beyond just "hello world" basics by including crucial real-world elements like debugging, JShell, the Scanner class, and string manipulation—all while staying accessible. The sections on Java control structures and primitive data types really stand out. They strike the perfect balance between theory and application, especially with how coding conventions and readability are emphasized. Also, the "learning while practicing" approach is more than a philosophy—it's embedded in the book's DNA.

– Joe Ghalbouni, Founder,
Learning While Practicing

Table of Contents

Preface

Welcome to *Java Essentials Volume 1: Programming Fundamentals*, a book thoughtfully written for those who are stepping into the world of Java with little to no prior experience. Whether you are an aspiring developer, a self-taught coder, a college freshman, or a high-school student eager to learn one of the most powerful and versatile programming languages in the world, this book was designed with you in mind.

Java has maintained its reputation as a reliable and universal language for over two decades—powering web servers, enterprise software, mobile apps, and even embedded devices. What makes Java stand out is not only its object-oriented structure but also its emphasis on readability, reliability, and portability. These are the very qualities that make Java an ideal first language for anyone learning how to program.

This volume begins by walking you through the practical steps of downloading, installing, and configuring the Java Development Kit (JDK) for your operating system. From there, you'll progress through the fundamentals of the language—writing your first program, using basic syntax, understanding primitive data types, handling user input, and exploring core topics such as control structures, operators, strings, and arrays.

Each chapter has been carefully crafted to build upon the last, integrating theory, annotated code samples, hands-on exercises, and review questions to reinforce your learning. You'll also encounter real-world programming practices, such as debugging compile-time and runtime errors, following Java coding conventions, and even using tools like JShell for interactive learning and experimentation.

What sets this book apart is its teaching philosophy: *learning while practicing*. Each topic is introduced gradually and reinforced with immediate application, ensuring that concepts are not just memorized but understood. As you complete each chapter, you'll gain more confidence in writing clean, logical, and well-structured Java programs.

This first volume lays the groundwork for more advanced Java topics, which will be explored in the second volume. By the end of this book, you will have acquired a solid foundation that prepares you for topics such as object-oriented design, exception handling, file I/O, collections, and GUI programming — all to be covered in *Java Essentials Volume 2: Object-Oriented Programming and Beyond*.

Thank you for choosing this book to begin your Java journey. Let's have your first Java cup together — coding one line at a time.

    Happy coding!

Michelle C. Decamora, MIT
Lawrence G. Decamora III, Ph.D

Introduction to the Book

Java Essentials Volume 1: Programming Fundamentals
is the first installment of a two-part series designed to
introduce new programmers to the fundamentals of the
Java programming language. Whether you are a student, an
aspiring developer, or someone simply curious about coding,
this volume will walk you through the essential building
blocks of Java in a clear and beginner-friendly manner.

In this volume, we begin by guiding you through the
process of downloading, installing, and configuring the Java
Development Kit (JDK) for different operating systems. You
will then write your first Java program, explore the structure
and syntax of the language, and learn how to handle user
input. We cover Java's primitive data types, operators,
control structures, and even delve into working with strings
and arrays—all crucial concepts for any Java programmer.

Our goal is to ensure that you gain a solid foundation in
Java, with a hands-on approach and practical examples
to reinforce every topic. Each chapter builds on the last,
creating a smooth and logical learning curve.

While this volume covers a wide range of beginner topics,
Java is a vast language, and there is more to explore
beyond the basics. *Java Essentials Volume 2: Object-Oriented
Programming and Beyond* picks up where this book leaves
off. In Volume 2, we explore object-oriented programming,
exception handling, file manipulation, graphical user
interfaces (GUIs), and more advanced features that will
deepen your understanding and broaden your skills in Java
development.

Thank you for choosing this book as your learning companion. We're excited to have you on this journey, and we hope you enjoy writing your first lines of Java code!

Let's begin!

Who Can Benefit From This Book?

This book is written with absolute beginners in mind—no prior programming experience is required. If you've never written a line of code before, *Java Essentials Volume 1: Programming Fundamentals* is the perfect starting point. It uses a gentle, structured approach to introduce you to Java in a way that's easy to follow and supported by real examples.

Here are some of the readers who will benefit most from this book:

- Aspiring software developers who want to learn Java as their first programming language.
- Self-taught learners and hobbyists who are curious about coding and want to explore Java at their own pace.
- Career switchers looking to transition into the tech industry and seeking a strong foundation in programming concepts using Java.
- High school or college educators who want a clear and structured resource for teaching Java to beginners.
- Technical professionals from other fields (like networking, engineering, or IT support) who wish to gain coding skills to complement their existing knowledge.
- Students enrolled in introductory programming courses who need a comprehensive, beginner-friendly reference for Java.

Whether you are reading this on your own, in a classroom, or as part of a training program, this book is designed to help you think like a programmer. The examples, exercises, and explanations are geared to make the learning experience as approachable and practical as possible.

If you're ready to build your first Java applications and understand the logic behind the code, then this book is for you.

How to Use This Book?

This book is designed to help you learn Java programming from the ground up. The content is organized in a way that supports gradual, hands-on mastery of the language. Here's how to make the most out of each chapter:

1. **Start with the Basics**

   Begin with Chapter 0, which walks you through downloading and installing the Java Development Kit (JDK) for your operating system. This ensures that your environment is ready for coding right from the start.

2. **Learn by Doing**

   Each chapter introduces concepts progressively and provides examples to help you practice what you've just learned. Be sure to type out and run the sample code — understanding comes faster through experimentation!

3. **Refer to Key Concepts**

   Look out for the following features throughout the book:

   - Tips for efficient coding and debugging
   - Code breakdowns explaining line-by-line logic
   - Common pitfalls so you can avoid typical beginner mistakes
   - Practical analogies to help relate abstract concepts to practical scenarios

4. Practice Regularly

Practice is the key to programming. Try to complete the exercises at the end of each chapter before moving on. You can also experiment by tweaking code samples and observing the effects. You can also try to answer the set of multiple-choice questions at the end of each chapter to help you evaluate what you've learned.

5. Use It As a Quick Reference

Once you've completed a chapter, feel free to revisit it whenever you need a refresher. Chapters are organized clearly, making it easy to find specific topics such as primitive data types, loops, or the Scanner class.

6. Explore Further in Volume 2

This volume focuses on the fundamental building blocks of Java. When you're ready to move into more advanced topics such as object-oriented programming, exception handling, file I/O, and GUIs, continue your learning journey with *Java Essentials Volume 2: Object-Oriented Programming and Beyond*.

7. Don't Rush

Java is a powerful language with many concepts to master. Take your time with each topic. Revisit tricky sections, seek clarification, and practice often. Learning to code is like learning a new language—it becomes easier with regular exposure and use.

8. Stay Curious

Programming is as much about problem-solving as it is about syntax. Don't just memorize — explore why things work the way they do. Use external documentation like the API Documentation, and engage with online communities if you hit a wall.

CHAPTER 0

Downloading, Installing, and Configuring the Java Development Kit (JDK)

Key Learning Objectives

- Know where to download the Java Development Kit (JDK)
- Install and configure the JDK
- Download and install your text editor
- Use the Java Compiler to compile a sample code
- Run a sample code

In Java, counting often starts at zero, so it only makes sense that our chapters do, too. Chapter 0 marks the true beginning: the foundation before the first method is called. This chapter will outline the key software you will need to learn Java – the JDK. You will know where to get the software and how to install and configure it on your specific computer, be it a Windows Machine, a Mac OS X, or a Linux Machine.

0.1 Where Do I Get My Java Development Kit (JDK)?

To download the Java Development Kit (JDK), you can search the internet using the search string "jdk <version> download".[1] Say you want to install JDK version 8, then you can search for "jdk 8 download." This book covers the up to JDK 23, but if you want to install the latest version, then you can just type "jdk download" into the Google search tab.

For beginners, it is best to use the latest JDK, but for users with older computers, if you have an operating system that still uses a 32-bit architecture, ie, for Windows XP, you should download JDK 1.8. Take a look at Figures 0.1 and 0.2 to see how a Google search result would look.

Figure 0.1 Google screenshot of the latest JDK installer to be downloaded

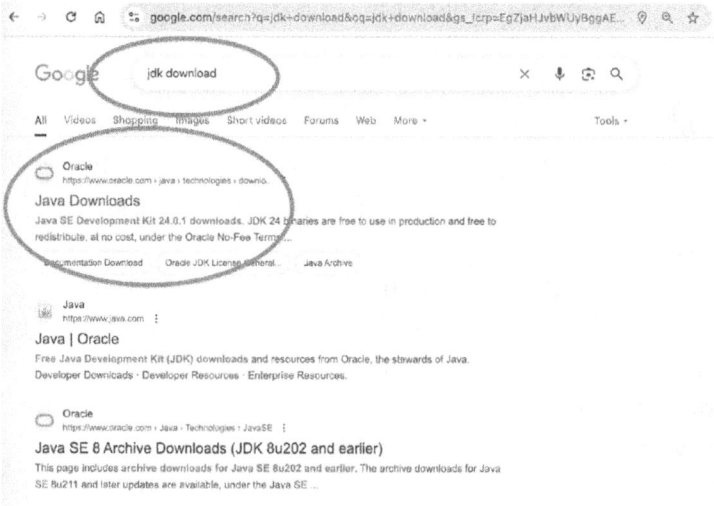

---

1. All syntax and search patterns are written in a separate font for better understanding.

Figure 0.2 Google screenshot of a specific JDK installer to be downloaded - JDK 1.8 installer

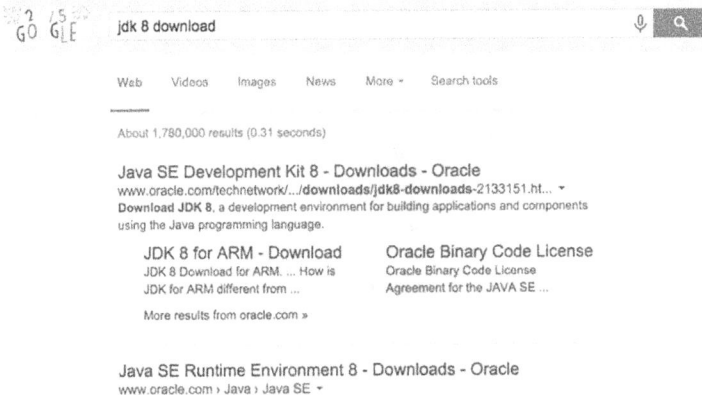

jdk 8 download

Web   Videos   Images   News   More ▾   Search tools

About 1,780,000 results (0.31 seconds)

Java SE Development Kit 8 - Downloads - Oracle
www.oracle.com/technetwork/.../downloads/jdk8-downloads-2133151.ht... ▾
Download JDK 8, a development environment for building applications and components
using the Java programming language.

JDK 8 for ARM - Download
JDK 8 Download for ARM. ... How is
JDK for ARM different from ...

Oracle Binary Code License
Oracle Binary Code License
Agreement for the JAVA SE ...

More results from oracle.com »

Java SE Runtime Environment 8 - Downloads - Oracle
www.oracle.com › Java › Java SE ▾

Google and the Google logo are trademarks of Google LLC.

Click on the Oracle® software link that you will see on your list of results, and it will redirect you to the download page on the Oracle website.

For older JDK versions, you might be asked to register on the Oracle developer website. You may be asked to accept a License Agreement if you want to download an archived JDK version. You need to click on the "**Accept License Agreement**" check box to allow the downloading of the JDK to continue.

Figure 0.3 Oracle Binary Code License Agreement

✕

You must accept the Oracle Binary Code License Agreement for the Java SE Platform Products to download this software.

☐ I reviewed and accept the Oracle Binary Code License Agreement for the Java SE Platform Products
Required

You will be redirected to the login screen in order to download the file.

Download jdk-8u202-macosx-x64.dmg ⬇

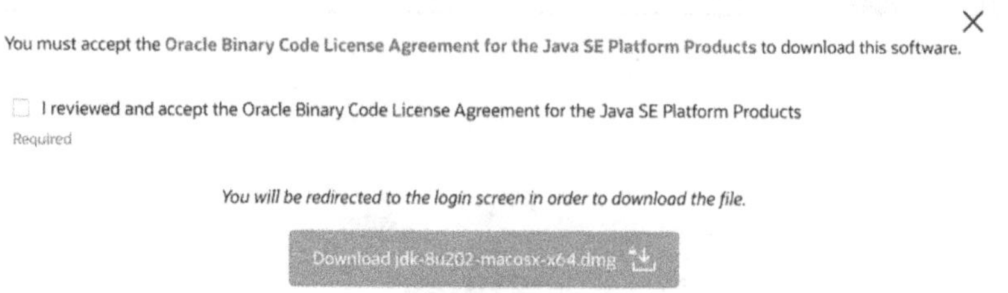

0.2 Downloading the Correct JDK For Your Machine

After agreeing to the license agreement by clicking the check box, the next step is to choose the correct installer for your machine. The list of JDK installers follows a certain pattern that will help you choose the correct installer. On the page below, you can choose the installers for a Linux OS, Mac OS, or Windows OS.

Figure 0.4 List of JDK Installers

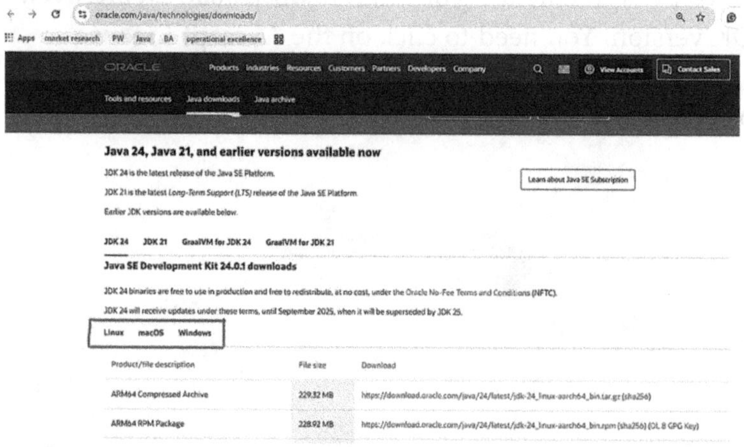

0.3 Installing the JDK in Mac OS X

Before installing your JDK, you need to check and satisfy your hardware requirements for your Mac OS X. You can install your JDK on any Intel-based computer (ie, iMac, MacBook, MacBook Air, MacBook Pro, etc.) or the newer Apple Silicon Chips (M1, M2, M3, or M4 chips).

To know what Mac OS version you are using, click on the "**Apple**" icon on the upper left part of the screen, then go to the "**About this Mac**" menu item. You will see the Mac OS version and the type of processor you are using, whether it is an Intel or an Apple Silicon Chip.

After learning about your Mac OS version, you also need to be sure that you have administrator privileges before you can install your JDK. If you don't have Mac OS X installed, you can either use a patch version of the JDK available on the internet called *soylatte*, or you can upgrade your OS.

When you have all the requirements, you can now start your JDK installation. When you install your Java Development Kit (JDK), the Java Runtime Environment (JRE) and the JavaFX SDK are installed and integrated into the standard JDK directory structure.

Depending on your processor, the downloaded file has one of the following names:

- For AMD processors, the name of your JDK installer is jdk-*version*u*update*-macosx-amd64.dmg.

- For Intel processors, the name of your JDK installer is jdk-*version*u*update*-macosx-x64.dmg.

- For JDK version 8, update 25, your installer's file name would probably be: jdk-8u25-macosx-amd64.dmg, for AMD and jdk-8u25-macosx-x64.dmg for Intel.

From either the Downloads window of the browser or from the file browser, you can now double-click the .dmg file to launch the installer. A Finder window will appear, containing an icon of an open box and the name of the .pkg file.

Figure 0.5 Mac OS Finder Window with the JDK .pkg file

Double-click the package icon to launch the Install app. The Install app displays the "**Introduction Screen.**" Just follow the instructions and use all the suggested default values by clicking "**Continue.**"

Figure 0.6 Mac OS JDK Installation Wizard

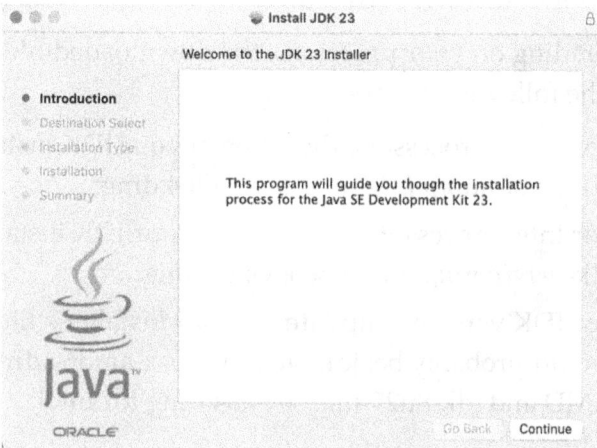

The "**Destination Select**" window will then appear. Just use the default suggestion of your installation wizard and click "**Continue**".

Figure 0.7 JDK Installation Wizard - Destination Select Part

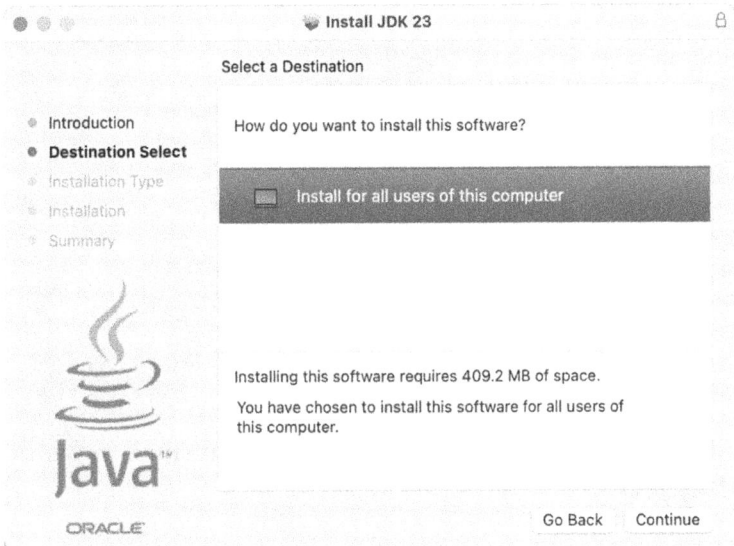

A window appears that has the message "**Installer is trying to install new software.**" You can either type your password to allow this to continue, or you can use your registered fingerprint, which will automatically enter the administrator login and password, and click **Install Software** to continue the installation process.

Figure 0.8 Password or Touch ID to continue the Installation Wizard

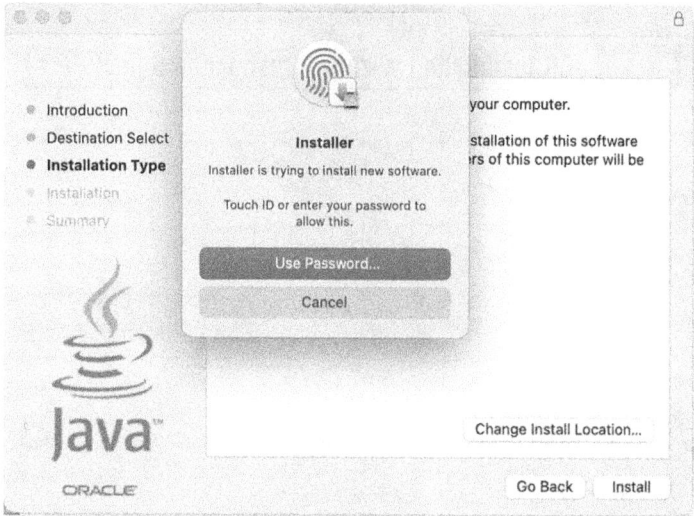

The software will be installed, and a confirmation window will appear.

Figure 0.9 Installation Succeeded

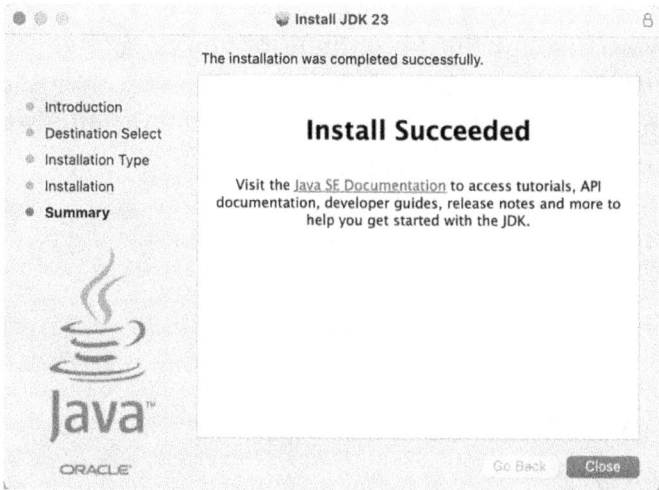

After the installation process is finished, you will be asked if you want to keep the installer saved on your disk or if you want to move it to Trash and discard it later permanently. By doing this, you will be able to save up on your disk space.

Figure 0.10 **JDK installer - To Keep or Move to Trash**

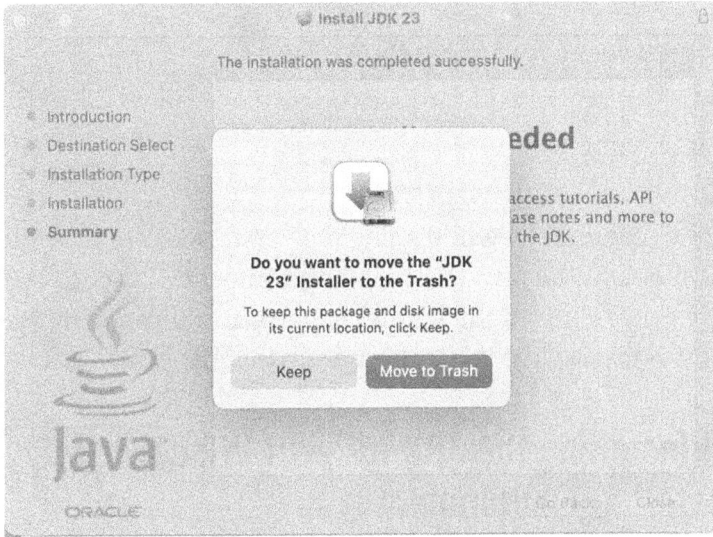

To test your compiler and to check your compiler's version, in your terminal window, type (without the % symbol): `javac -version`.

Figure 0.11 **Mac OS Finder Window - Checking the javac command**

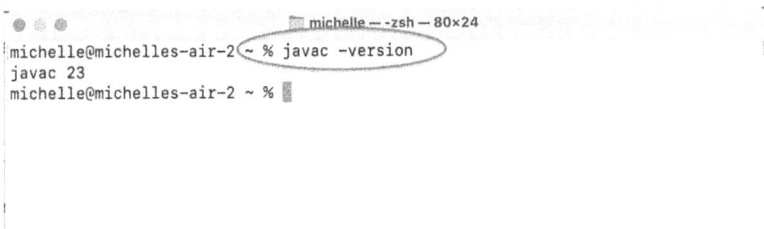

To test your Java Runtime command, type (without the %):
`java -version`

Figure 0.12 Mac OS Finder Window - Checking the Java command

```
● ● ●                    michelle — -zsh — 80×24
michelle@michelles-air-2 ~ % javac -version
javac 23
michelle@michelles-air-2 ~ % java -version
java version "23" 2024-09-17
Java(TM) SE Runtime Environment (build 23+37-2369)
Java HotSpot(TM) 64-Bit Server VM (build 23+37-2369, mixed mode, sharing)
michelle@michelles-air-2 ~ % ▌
```

Both commands will display the versions of both the Java compiler and the Java Runtime Environment. It should be fairly easy to install the JDK on a Mac OS Environment. It requires minimal to no configuration in most cases.

0.4 Installing the JDK for your Windows Operating Environment

Follow the steps below to install the JDK for your Windows Operating Environment.

0.4.1 Check the JDK for your Windows Operating Environment

To check if your Windows OS has a pre-installed JDK, try opening your Command Prompt by pressing the Windows Key and typing CMD. In your command prompt, type `javac` in the prompt as shown in the screenshot below.

| Figure 0.13 | Windows Command Prompt - checking the javac command |

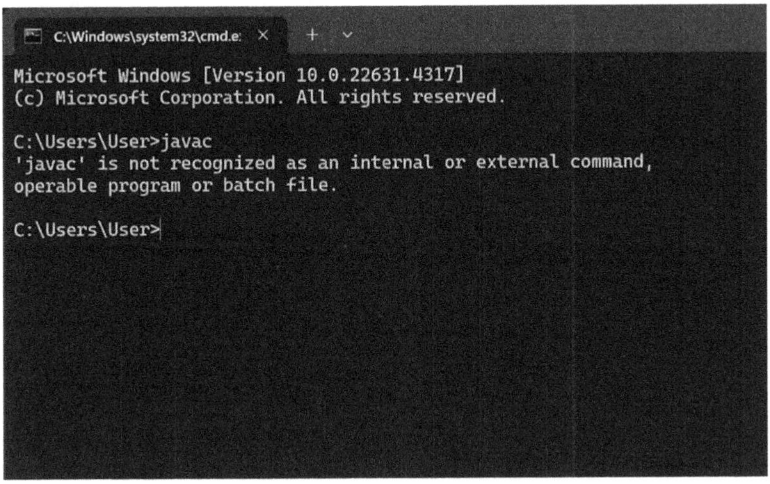

```
C:\Windows\system32\cmd.e:  ×    +  ∨
Microsoft Windows [Version 10.0.22631.4317]
(c) Microsoft Corporation. All rights reserved.

C:\Users\User>javac
'javac' is not recognized as an internal or external command,
operable program or batch file.

C:\Users\User>
```

If it shows that it does not recognize the `javac` command, then you may need to start the downloading, installing, and configuration process of your JDK on your Windows OS.

0.4.2 Download the JDK for your Windows Operating Environment

Do a Google search: `JDK download` as shown in the image below.

| Figure 0.14 | Google Screenshot of the latest JDK installer to be downloaded |

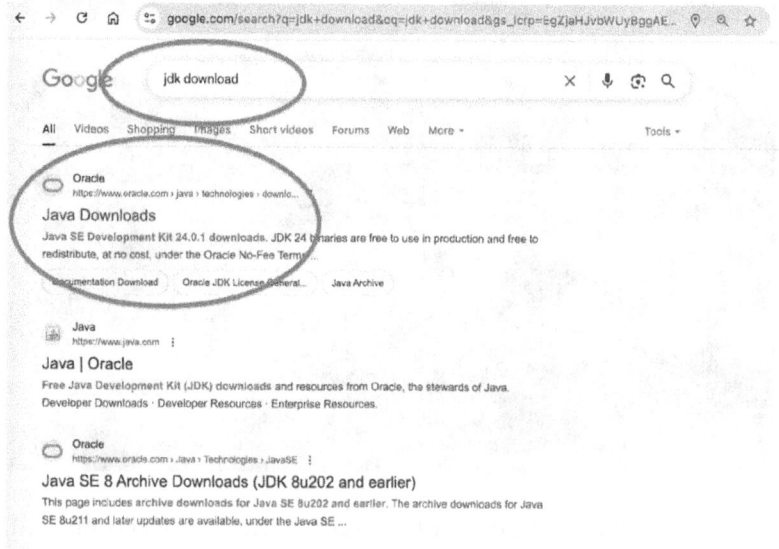

Google and the Google logo are trademarks of Google LLC.

Click the first Oracle website link related to your search. It's better to get the JDK from the source, which is the official Oracle website.

Figure 0.15 Available JDK Installers for the Windows OS

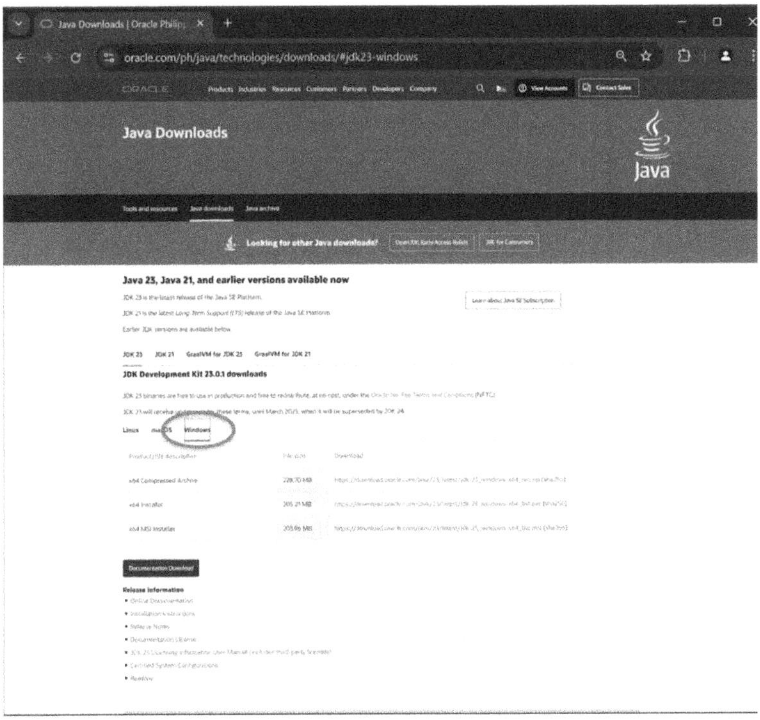

Choose **"Windows"** from the options (Linux, Mac OS, Windows). Choose x64 Installer if you are using an Intel-based machine. The downloaded installer will be saved in the Downloads folder, as shown below.

Figure 0.16 JDK 23 Windows Installer inside the Downloads Folder

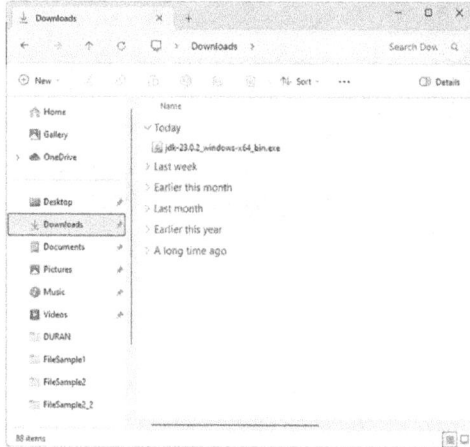

0.4.3 Install the JDK in your Windows Operating Environment

After you have downloaded your JDK, be sure that you have administrative permissions to install the JDK on Microsoft Windows. You can start the installation process by double-clicking the installer. This will start the JDK installation wizard, as shown below.

Figure 0.17 JDK 23 Windows Installer Installation Wizard

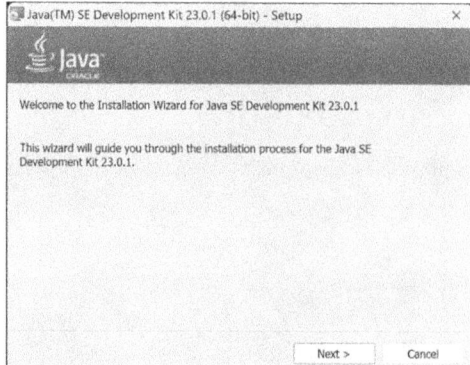

If this is your first time installing the JDK, it is better to follow the default values provided by the installation wizard by clicking **Next** until it finishes the installation process. After the installation is finished, you can check your "Program Files\Java" folder, you will see that a jdk-<version> folder is created. In this case, since we installed JDK 23, you will see the jdk-23 folder.

0.4.4 Configure your JDK for the Windows OS

After a successful installation, the next step is to configure the following environment variables on your Windows Operating System. These are the following environment variables: CLASSPATH, JAVA_HOME, and Path.

The CLASSPATH in the Windows OS is an environment variable that tells the Java Virtual Machine (JVM) and Java compiler where to look for user-defined classes and packages when running Java applications. It specifies the directories or JAR files that contain compiled Java classes that are needed by the application. To start setting the environment variables, open your File Explorer and right-click on "**This PC,**" which is found on the left panel.

Figure 0.18 File Explorer

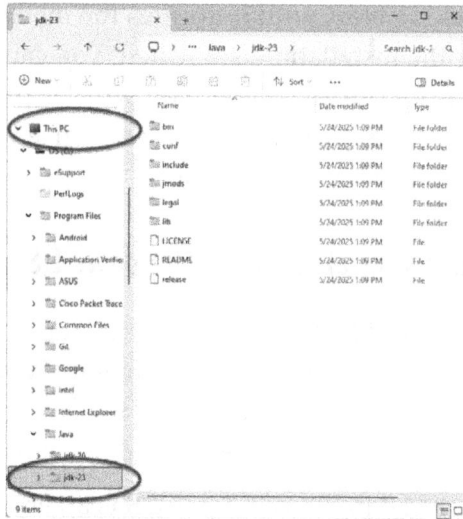

Choose the **"Properties"** option. This will open the **"System Properties"** of your Windows Environment as shown below.

Figure 0.19 Properties Window

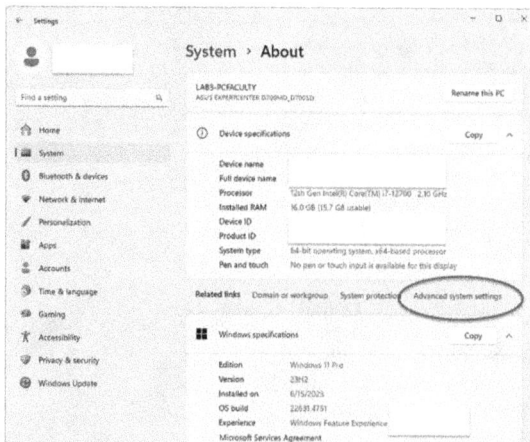

Choose **"Advanced system settings"**.

Figure 0.20 System Property Window

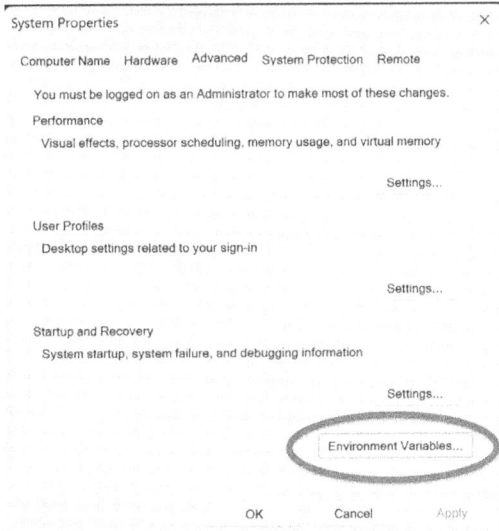

Choose **"Environment Variables"**.

Figure 0.21 Environment Variable Window

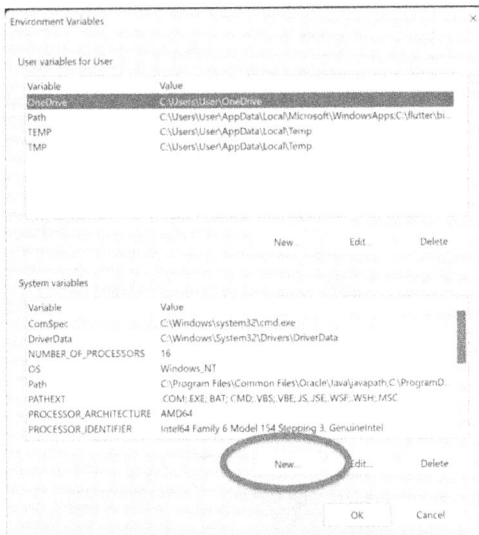

Click the "**New...**" button under the "**System variables**" so that you can start adding new environment variables like the CLASSPATH and the JAVA_HOME.

In the "**Variable Name**", type in: CLASSPATH, then in "**Variable Value**" type in "." (period only) as shown below. Click OK to close the window.

Figure 0.22 Environment Variable Window - Entering CLASSPATH

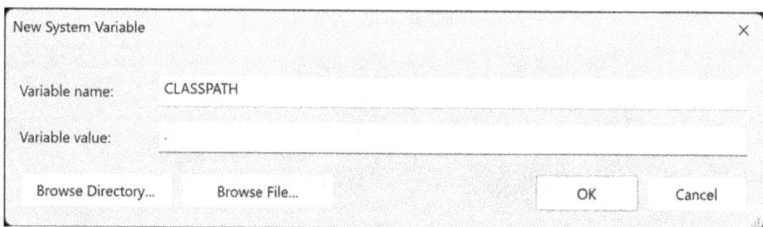

New System Variable				×
Variable name:	CLASSPATH			
Variable value:	.			
Browse Directory...	Browse File...		OK	Cancel

Next, we will set the JAVA_HOME variable. Follow the same procedure, click the '**New...**' button under the '**System variables**' so that you can start adding new environment variables; this time, we will add the JAVA_HOME variable as shown below.

Figure 0.23 Environment Variable Window - Entering JAVA_HOME

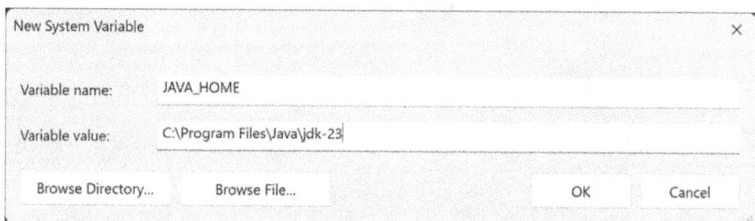

New System Variable				×
Variable name:	JAVA_HOME			
Variable value:	C:\Program Files\Java\jdk-23			
Browse Directory...	Browse File...		OK	Cancel

In order to lessen the possibility of mistyping any value of the environment variables, it will be better to copy+paste it from the source. The "**Variable Value**" should be copied from the actual location.

Open the File Explorer, go to the `C:\Program Files\Java\jdk-23` folder, and do an actual copy+paste on the address bar as shown below.

Figure 0.24 **File Explorer - Java Home Folder**

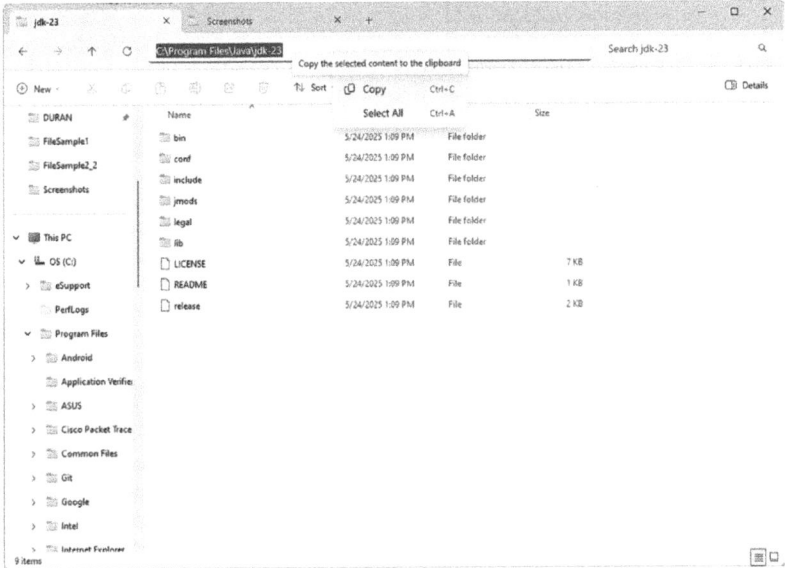

Use the value copied from the address bar for the variable value of your JAVA_HOME environment variable.

After setting your CLASSPATH and your JAVA_HOME, it's time to edit the Path.

This time, under the System Variables Window, instead of choosing "**New...**", choose "**Edit...**". This will open up the "**Environment Variables**" window as shown below. Click the **New** button found on the upper left part of the window, then input the following: %JAVA_HOME%\bin. Be sure that there are no extra spaces in the text you entered. After that, press **OK** to close the Window.

Figure 0.25 Environment Variable - Edit `Path`

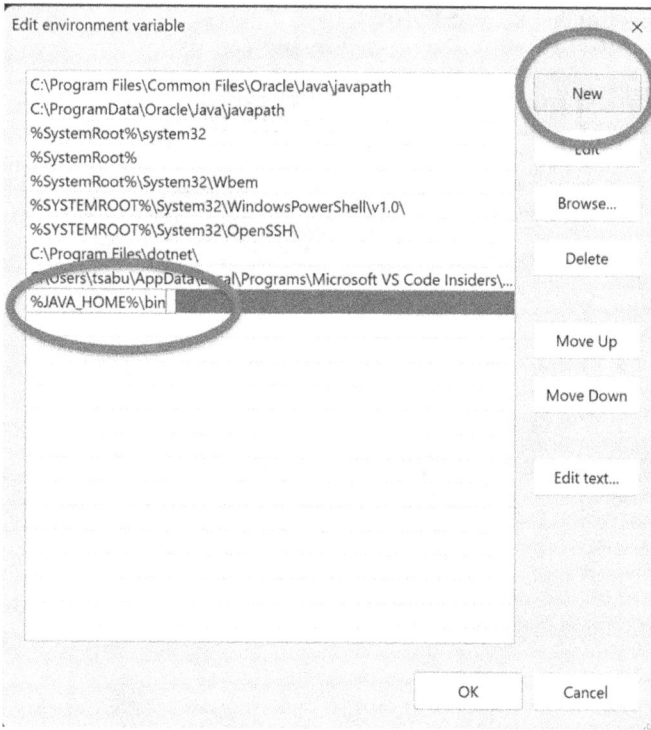

The %JAVA_HOME%\bin is a path notation used in Windows to refer to the bin directory within the Java installation folder. Let's dissect %JAVA_HOME%\bin.

- **%JAVA_HOME%:** This is an environment variable that points to the root directory of the Java Development Kit (JDK) installation. It usually contains the path where Java is installed (for example, C:\Program Files\Java\jdk-23).

- **\bin:** The bin folder inside the Java installation directory contains essential Java executables, such as java (the Java Runtime), javac (the Java compiler), and other tools like jshell.

0.4.5 Test JDK on Your Windows Machine

Close all existing Command Prompts; you don't need them. You have to open a new one so that the newly added environment variables on your Windows Operating System will take effect. Let us open a new command prompt and type in `javac -version` as shown below.

Figure 0.26 Command Prompt - Testing the javac command

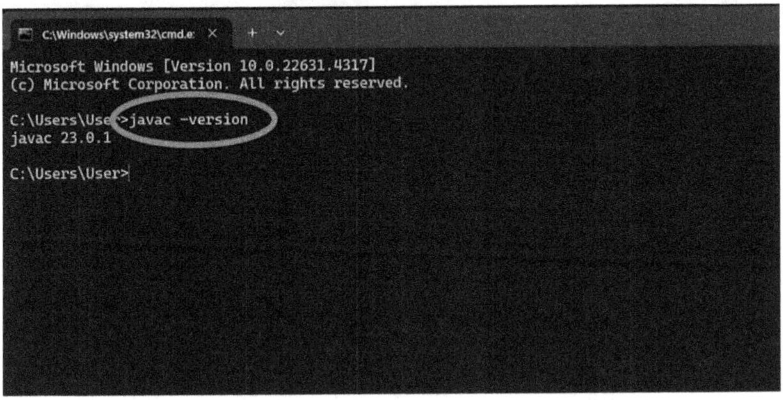

This will show that your compiler is working and that the version of your Java compiler is version 23. Next, type in `java -version` to test your Java Runtime Environment, as shown below.

Figure 0.27 Command Prompt - Testing the Java command

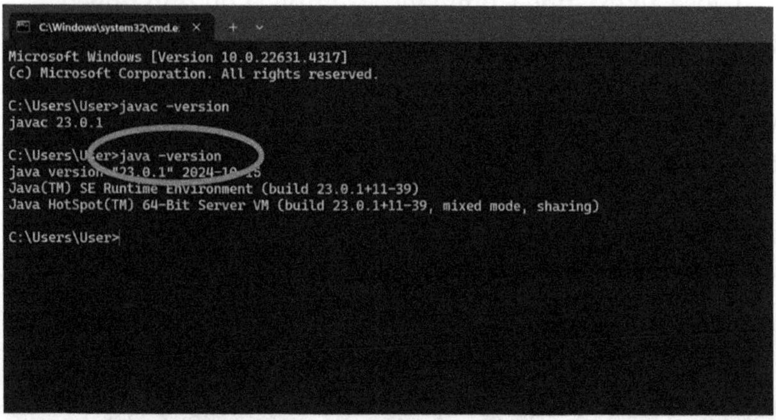

0.5 JDK Installer for Linux Operating Environment

In the Linux Operating Environment, there are two types of users: root users and regular users. The root users have access to all the folders of your Linux machine, while the regular users have access only to their home folder. Knowing what type of user account you have will help you decide what type of JDK Linux installer you can download.

There are two file types you can choose from: the *.tar. gz file or archive binaries, and the *.rpm file or the *red hat package manager* file. There is also a special installer available for Intel machines that uses the Linux distribution. Below is the list of available Linux installers.

Figure 0.28 Oracle Site - Linux JDK Installers

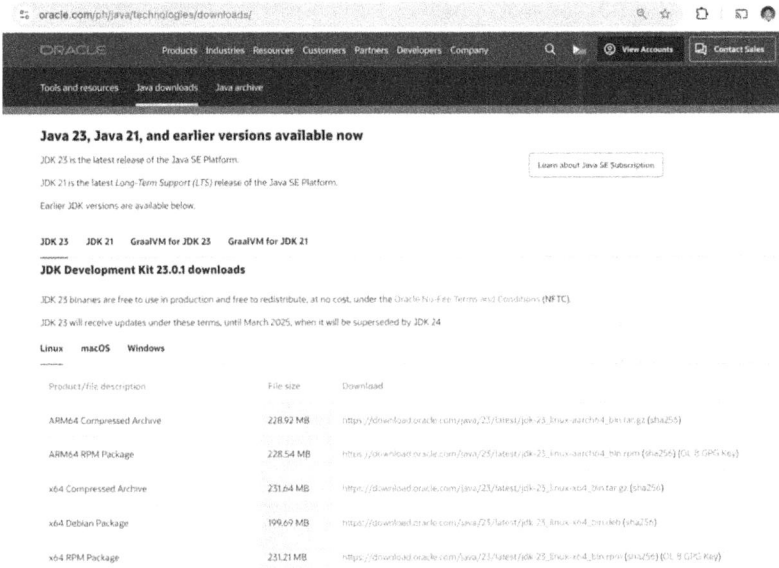

0.5.1 The Archive Binaries (*.tar.gz)

The archive binaries can be used by any type of user, both regular and root users. Using the archived binaries, you can choose the location where you can extract the files. After choosing where to extract the installer, you may start the extraction process by typing:

```
% tar zxvf jdk-<version>u<update>-linux-x64.tar.gz
```

Assuming you want to extract your JDK inside the home folder, here is an example of the actual command, assuming the installer is JDK 23.

```
\% cd <ENTER>
% tar zxvf jdk-23_linux-x64_bin.tar.gz <ENTER>
```

The first command ensures that your present working directory will be the home folder, while the second command extracts the JDK inside your home folder.

Also, with the tar command, you can extract the said installer inside the home folder.

The next step is to configure your JDK by editing the file .profile. You can use the vi editor or any text editor to edit the .profile file.

Add the lines:

```
JAVA_HOME=~/jdk-23
export JAVA_HOME
PATH=$JAVA_HOME/bin:$PATH
export PATH
```

Save your .profile.

Log out and log in again on your machine.

0.5.2 The RedHat Package Manager (RPM) File

The RPM file is intended to be used by root users for package installation. You may download the JDK installer with the *.rpm extension name.

After downloading the file, you need to log in as the root user by using the su command. Here's a sample command.

```
%su -
<Type in your root password>
#
```

After logging in as root, you can now execute your rpm command to start installing the package.

```
# rpm -Uvh jdk-23_linux-x64_bin.rpm <ENTER>
```

After the installation, you can log out as root back to a regular user, and you're done. No need to restart your machine. Remember that installers that contain the x64 value in the name of the installer are for Intel-based processors. For other types of processors, you can use the ARM64 installer.

Chapter Summary

- There are different types of computers running different types of Operating Systems. The first crucial step is to know the type of your operating system, and then do a Google search for the right JDK to be installed.

- For 64-bit operating systems, it is recommended to use the latest JDK version.

- For older operating systems, you can use JDK 8, available to serve any 32-bit Windows or Linux operating system.

- Once you've properly installed and configured your JDK, you need to know what version you're using by typing in `javac -version` to know the Java compiler's version and `java -version` to know the runtime environment's version.

- Ideally, it is better to have the same version for your compiler (`javac`) and your runtime (`java`), but if for some reason they're not, be sure that your `javac` has a lower version than your `java` version.

Quiz

1. **Which of the following IS NOT an Operating System?**
   a. Windows
   b. Linux
   c. MacOSX
   d. JDK

2. **Which of the following statements is NOT TRUE?**
   a. For Mac OS, there's no need to install the JDK, all Mac OS versions have a pre-installed JDK.
   b. For older Windows OS, JDK 8 is the best JDK version because it still has both the 32-bit and 64-bit versions.
   c. For a modern OS, it is best to use the latest JDK version.
   d. To get the latest JDK version, just Google search "JDK download"

3. **To know the Java Compiler's version, the command is:**
   a. `javac -version`
   b. `javac -v`
   c. `compiler -v`
   d. `java compiler -v`

4. **To know the Java Runtime Environment version, the command is:**
   a. `java -runtime`
   b. `java -r`
   c. `java -version`
   d. `java -run`

5. A dmg type of installer is for what Operating System?

   a. Windows
   b. Linux
   c. MacOSX
   d. Any OS

6. An exe type of installer is for what Operating System?

   a. Windows
   b. Linux
   c. MacOSX
   d. Any OS

7. A tar.gz type of installer is for what Operating System?

   a. Windows
   b. Linux
   c. MacOSX
   d. Any OS

8. A Linux rpm file installer is also an alternative file type of installer for Linux machines. What does rpm stand for?

   a. Revolutions per minute
   b. Rotations per minute
   c. RedHat package manager
   d. Recovery per minute

9. **Which of the following statements is NOT TRUE?**

   a. RPM Linux installers are best used by root users only.

   b. It is best to know the admin password of your Windows Machine when configuring the `Path`, `CLASSPATH`, and `JAVA_HOME` environment variables.

   c. Regular Linux OS users can install JDK by using the tar.gz file installer.

   d. The hardest JDK installation can be experienced on a Mac OS Machine.

10. **Which of the following statements is NOT TRUE?**

    a. The JDK can run, but it must be properly installed and configured first.

    b. The installation process for a root user for a Linux machine typically uses a tar.gz installer.

    c. The installation process in a Windows operating system is almost the same regardless of the Windows OS version.

    d. The Mac OS installer uses a `dmg` file.

Answers

1 – d	2 – a	3 – a	4 – c	5 – c
6 – a	7 – b	8 – c	9 – d	10 – b

JDK Installation Task

Ensure that you have installed and configured your JDK on your local machine.

CHAPTER 1

Your First Java Cup

Key Learning Objectives

- Identify the key features that make Java a popular, modern, and powerful programming language.
- Understand the three core technology flavors of Java: Java SE, Java EE (Jakarta EE), and Java ME.
- Differentiate between the Java Development Kit (JDK) and the Java Runtime Environment (JRE).
- Explain the role of Java's automatic memory management system, the Garbage Collector.
- Describe how Java helps ensure code security through three built-in protective tasks.

In this chapter, you will take your first sip from the Java cup by getting acquainted with the foundational concepts that define the language. Java has remained one of the most widely used programming languages in the world, thanks to its reliability, versatility, and strong community support. You'll begin by exploring the key features that make Java unique, from platform independence to object-oriented design. Then you'll

learn about the different "flavors" of Java that cater
to desktop, enterprise, and embedded applications.
As you move forward in this chapter, you'll discover
the critical differences between the JDK and JRE—two
essential components in any Java programmer's toolkit.
You'll also be introduced to Java's automatic memory
management system, the Garbage Collector, and how it
simplifies resource handling. Finally, we'll discuss how
Java's architecture is designed with built-in mechanisms
that enhance code security. These topics will provide
the essential groundwork for everything you'll learn in
the rest of the book.

1.1 The Key Features of Java

Have you ever wondered why, in today's technology
and after all these years, we still study Java? The following
timeless key features are the reason why Java is still relevant.

1.1.1 Java is Object-Oriented

Java is an object-oriented programming language.
Object-oriented programming (OOP) is a way of writing
programs by organizing code into "objects," which represent
real-world things like a car, a person, or a bank account.
Each object contains *data* (called attributes) and *behaviors*
(called methods) that define what it is and what it can do.
This approach makes code easier to understand, reuse, and
maintain.

Object-oriented programming languages support
three main features: **Encapsulation**, **Inheritance**, and
Polymorphism.

1. **Encapsulation:** allows you to protect your data from direct access. It also provides a common interface that makes it accessible and guards the state of your data by checking the correctness of the values assigned before updating the value. It also allows you to create methods that can be called later in your code, and the users or callers of those methods need not worry about how the method was implemented. In getting information, the user will just need to call the getter methods, whereas, for changing a value or a state of an object, the user just needs to call the setter methods. These setter and getter methods, as we call them, are responsible for accessing and updating the `private` variables in the class that are protected from any direct access.

2. **Inheritance:** on the other hand, is a way to reuse objects, carrying over what was already created and allowing added methods and attributes to be written on top of what you already have. This useful feature allows programmers to reuse what was already coded without making them rewrite code and produce redundancies. Reusing code can make the runtime of your application faster by eliminating duplicate code.

3. **Polymorphism:** is another process that will allow you to change the method implementation during runtime by having a certain declared type of class and implementing the methods of the subtype (subclass), also known as Virtual Method Invocation (VMI). A discussion on classes and VMI will be made available in *Java Essentials Volume 2: Object-Oriented Programming and Beyond.*

An object-oriented programming language must have these three main features. We need these features so that we can create programs that are patterned to real-life objects, like dates and buttons, and code that we can reuse.

These objects may interact with other objects, like a Student object that can interact with a Teacher object. Another thing about object-oriented programming is its capability to reuse code, not just by using inheritance but also by creating independent code (loosely coupled code). You can create an object that will be used in a certain project and reuse it in another. For example, if you have a Student object being used in a desktop application, you can reuse the same object for a web application as well.

Here's another example. In a banking application, you write code that represents a bank customer name in a Customer class. This Customer class can be reused in other applications not related to the said banking project. Say you have an Order and Purchasing System. You don't have to reinvent the wheel or rewrite the Customer class code. What you can do is to reuse them in both the Banking System and the Order and Purchasing Systems.

1.1.2 Java is Simple

Most of the Java format was based on C and C++, so if you are a C or C++ programmer, migrating to Java would be very easy. C, C++, and Java share almost all programming formats.

Java made it easier for C and C++ programmers to absorb the concepts of pointers. Instead of pointers, Java uses the concept of references. These topics will be discussed in detail in Volume 2 of this series.

1.1.3 Java is Robust

Java is a strict, highly disciplined programming language. It deals with clear errors and enables you to trap exceptions, and has no ambiguous structure. Everything is clear in Java, including its syntax, rules, and structure. It clearly deals with and handles exceptions and displays clear error messages that are beneficial to programmers whenever they debug their code.

1.1.4 Java is Multi-Threaded

Java applications can run several threads, sometimes called sub-processes or parallel processes. A thread is a virtual CPU, which is similar to a virtual machine. It contains three things: the virtual CPU, the code, and the data.

Multi-threading makes use of these three elements and creates its own independent runtime process inside a running Java application. It is extremely useful in practice. For example, a browser should be able to simultaneously download multiple images while accessing other data storage devices or printing a document. Another example is a web server. It needs to be able to serve concurrent requests, and each request that it serves is another thread process.

Multithreading and Multitasking are somewhat similar, as both are managed by the underlying Operating System (OS). Multi-tasking is the ability of the OS to manage multiple concurrent applications that run on top of the OS, while multi-threading is the process of managing each smaller process (also known as threads) that runs in a single application.

Figure 1.1 illustrates Java's multithreading capability, where multiple threads can run concurrently within a single Java program to handle different tasks like the graphical user interface, database access, and printing. Each thread operates independently, allowing the application to be more responsive and efficient by performing tasks in parallel.

A Java GUI Application can update the database while printing and updating the record on the GUI display is an example of a multi-threaded application.

Figure 1.1 Multithreading diagram on a sample application

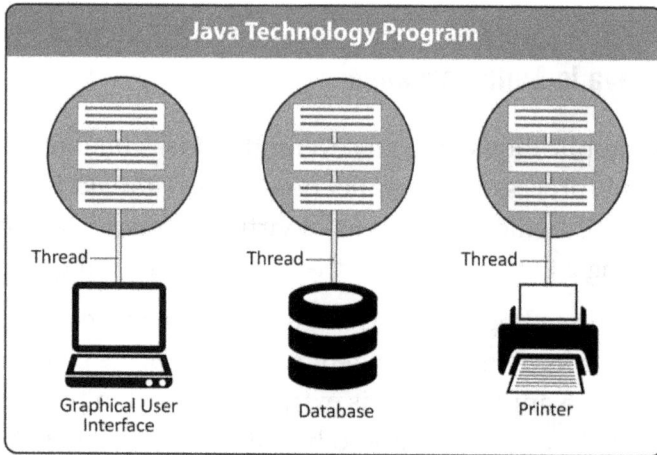

However, Java 21 introduces *Virtual Threads* — a groundbreaking feature that dramatically simplifies the task of creating and managing threads, especially when compared to the traditional platform threads used in older Java versions.

In older Java versions, each thread was tied directly to an operating system (OS) thread, which meant creating thousands of concurrent threads was resource-intensive and could quickly overwhelm the system due to memory and CPU constraints. Managing such threads also required careful tuning, the use of thread pools, and asynchronous programming models that added complexity to codebases.

With Java 21's Virtual Threads, Java applications can now create millions of lightweight threads that are not bound to OS threads. These virtual threads are managed by the Java Virtual Machine (JVM) itself, allowing them to be suspended and resumed efficiently without blocking system resources. As a result, developers can write simple, blocking-style code (e.g., using `Thread.sleep()` or waiting on I/O) without the performance penalty traditionally associated with it. This means clearer, more maintainable code without the need for complex concurrency frameworks or callback hell.

In summary, Java 21's virtual threads make concurrent programming far more scalable, efficient, and beginner-friendly, offering the simplicity of synchronous code with the scalability of asynchronous execution.

1.1.5 Java is Network Aware

The Java programming language was created so that users of this language can write applications that can share information through most types of networks.

Java programmers can write client-server applications that can run on most types of networks. A Java-based server application can run on one physical machine, while another browser-based client can request information and run on a different machine. At some point, Java was called the Internet Programming Language, which allows developers to create applications that run on the web.

1.1.6 Java Ensures Cross-Platform Compatibility

Java can run on most popular platforms. This feature is valuable to a lot of customers who have invested in hardware like minicomputers, mainframes, or even desktop computers. They do not want to do away with these investments when they use another set of standards.

One of the nice things about Java is its capability to run on most platforms once you are done with the compilation and archiving. Once you compile your source file (`*.java`), it produces a compiled file (`*.class`) which contains your Java bytecode. Then you can let your `*.class` run in any Java Runtime Environment on any platform. In most instances, a single Java source file can produce several class files. In cases like this, having multiple class files is very hard to manage and to deliver to clients. This is where a JAR file comes in handy. JAR stands for Java **AR**chive. It allows the grouping of related classes together to form a single archived file called a JAR File.

Having a single JAR File will allow users to execute and manage a program more easily compared to having multiple, scattered class files.

As shown in Figure 1.2, Java source files (*.java) are compiled into bytecode (*.class), which can then be packaged into a *.jar file and executed by the Java Virtual Machine (JVM). Since the JVM is available on various platforms like Windows, Mac OS, Linux OS, and Solaris, the same Java program can run seamlessly across all these systems, demonstrating Java's cross-platform capability.

Figure 1.2 **Cross-platform diagram on Java Virtual Machine**

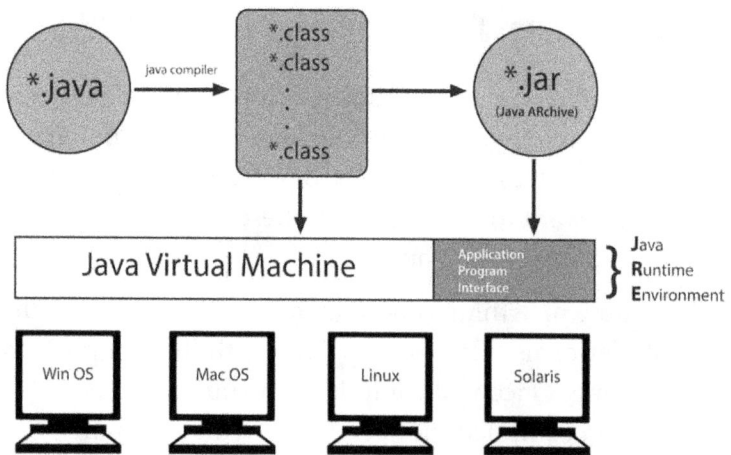

Say, you wrote your source file in a Windows Operating System. You then compiled and tested it. This Windows-based application that you wrote using Java was used for a year or two. Then another set of hardware machines was purchased, but this time it was using a better operating system, say the Linux OS. Would you still be able to use your Windows-based Java application? The answer is yes! All you need to do is install the needed Java Runtime Environment on your Linux machine and voila! Your Java Application that used to run on Windows should also be able to run on your Linux machine.

1.1.7 Java is Secure

Java Applications are secured because they run on top of the Java Virtual Machine (JVM). The JVM is one of the components of your Java Runtime Environment (JRE), which allows you to run Java bytecodes on your platform. Java bytecodes are inside your class files and your JAR files. Once you have installed your JRE, you're all set. You can now run your Java Application on your machine.

Your JVM interprets the compiled Java code (`*.class`) and runs it. Your JVM sits on top of your operating system and acts as its boundary; this means your running Java application cannot perform any disruptive actions that are not approved by your boundary setter—your JVM. Having this additional layer also means that your Java application does not have a direct attachment or a direct contact with your underlying operating system; it needs to go through a series of layers before it reaches your Operating System. So, whatever transaction you have running on top of your JVM (which is your Java App), your underlying Operating System cannot directly access it. Java does not allow direct access to memory; this makes it impossible to accidentally reference memory that belongs to other programs or the kernel.

Figure 1.3 shows how a Java application (historically, applets embedded in web pages) sent from a server is blocked from executing on the client side due to the secure design of the Java Virtual Machine (JVM). The JVM acts as a boundary between the Java application and the underlying operating system, preventing direct access to system memory and unauthorized actions, which enhances security by requiring all operations to go through controlled layers.

Figure 1.3 Applications are not directly installed on the OS Level

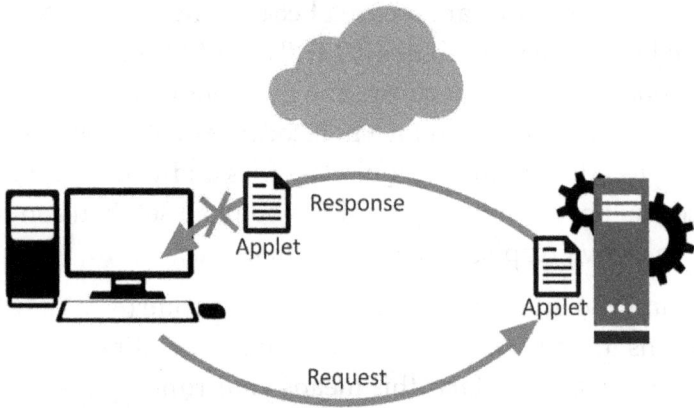

Also, Java SE has its own set of API (Application Program Interfaces) that allow programmers to use pre-created code and classes by the Java Developer Community. It is also an essential part of the JRE. Java security technology includes tools, implementations of commonly used security algorithms, mechanisms, and protocols. The Java Security API spans a wide range of areas, including cryptography, public key infrastructure, secure communications, authentication, and access control. It also provides the user or administrator with a set of tools to securely manage applications.

1.1.8 Java Supports GUI

Using Java, you can also create Graphical User Interface (GUI) Applications, which enable the user to make use of `Buttons`, `Frames`, `TextFields`, and other graphical objects that you can use in creating your user interface. Java Foundation Classes (JFC) is one of the most popular graphical frameworks used by Java for building portable GUI applications. JFC consists of the Abstract Window Toolkit (AWT), Swing, and Java 2D, which, in combination, can produce a GUI that can run in most types of Operating Systems.

Figure 1.4 Sample output of a simple GUI notepad

In JFC, you can customize the look and feel of your GUI application, and it has a wide range of GUI components that you can choose from. In the sample GUI Notepad image provided in Figure 1.4, you can see that I can create my own simple GUI notepad application that Java also supports.

JavaFX is an open-source, next-generation client application platform for desktop, mobile, and embedded systems built on Java.

1.1.9 Java is Free

The Java Development Kit (JDK) and the Java Runtime Environment (JRE) installers can be downloaded from the Oracle website at no cost. It is free for personal and academic use.

1.2 The Three Flavors of Java

The term "**Three Flavors of Java**" refers to the three main editions of the Java platform, each tailored to different types of development environments and applications.

Each of these editions serves a distinct purpose, ensuring that Java can be applied across a wide range of development scenarios, from simple desktop applications to complex enterprise systems and embedded devices.

Figure 1.5 **The Java Technology Family**

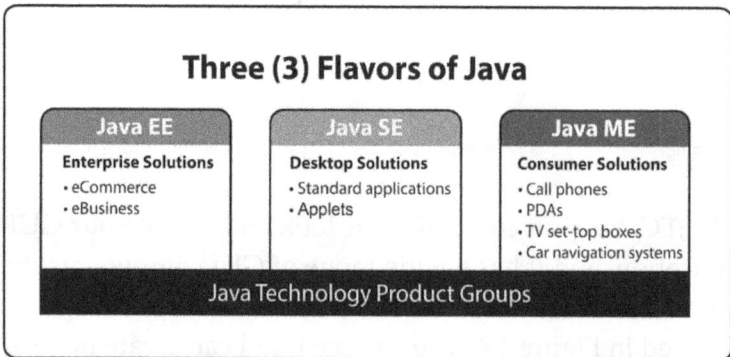

Three (3) Flavors of Java

Java EE	Java SE	Java ME
Enterprise Solutions	**Desktop Solutions**	**Consumer Solutions**
• eCommerce	• Standard applications	• Call phones
• eBusiness	• Applets	• PDAs
		• TV set-top boxes
		• Car navigation systems

Java Technology Product Groups

In the good old days, it used to be J2ME, J2SE, and J2EE, but as of version 6.0, Sun Microsystems (the original developer of Java technology, which is now owned by Oracle Corporation) decided to rebrand their technology as Java SE, Java EE, and Java ME. Let's look at each of these three technologies in detail.

1.2.1 Java SE (Standard Edition)

Java SE contains the standard class libraries that can be used to create applets and/or desktop applications. It is the core of all Java-based technology. `Applets` were deprecated starting JDK 9.

Java SE is the core platform, providing essential libraries and APIs for developing general-purpose applications, such as desktop applications and command-line utilities. It includes key packages like `java.lang`, `java.util`, and `java.io`, along with GUI toolkits like `AWT`, `Swing`, and `JavaFX`.

1.2.2 Java EE (Enterprise Edition)

Java EE is a framework that allows developers to use vendor-neutral technologies in developing their enterprise applications. Java EE makes use of the standard libraries and other extended API's (Application Programming Interface) in building and deploying these applications, and it usually makes use of the browsers as its client and can be used by multiple, concurrent users. Java EE is a widely used platform for server programming and provides functionality to deploy fault-tolerant, multi-tier, distributed Java technology applications based largely on modular components running on an application server.

1.2.3 Java ME (Micro Edition)

Java ME, on the other hand, is a stripped-down version of the standard library of Java SE; it is designed for embedded systems for small devices. The target device may range from industrial control devices to mobile phones to tablets and set-top boxes, and other embedded devices.

Java ME is a lightweight version of Java, specifically crafted for devices with limited resources, such as mobile phones, embedded systems, and IoT (Internet of Things) devices. It provides a subset of Java SE and adds APIs for smaller devices, making it ideal for developing applications on systems with constrained memory, processing power, and screen size.

Figure 1.6 shows how Java ME, Java SE, and Java EE interact with one another.

Figure 1.6 The relationship of each Java technology flavor

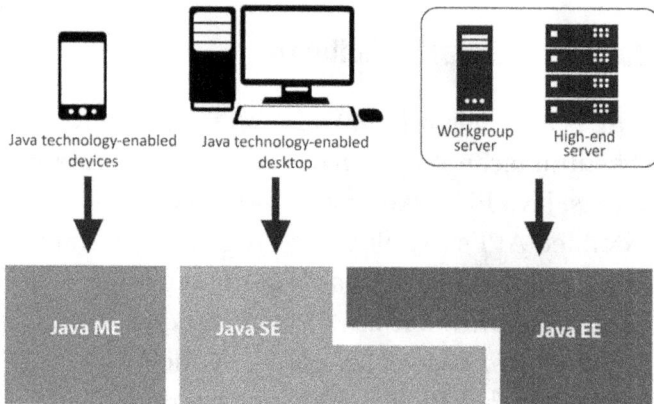

Java EE, now known as Jakarta EE, builds on Java SE and is designed for large-scale, distributed, multi-tiered enterprise applications. It includes everything from Java SE

and adds powerful APIs for building web services, handling servlets and JSP, managing enterprise beans (EJB), and working with technologies like JPA (Java Persistence API) and JMS (Java Message Service). Java EE is commonly used for web applications and back-end services in enterprise environments.

Figure 1.7 shows the relationship between Java SE, sometimes called Core Java, and Java EE.

Figure 1.7 The relationship of Java SE and Java EE

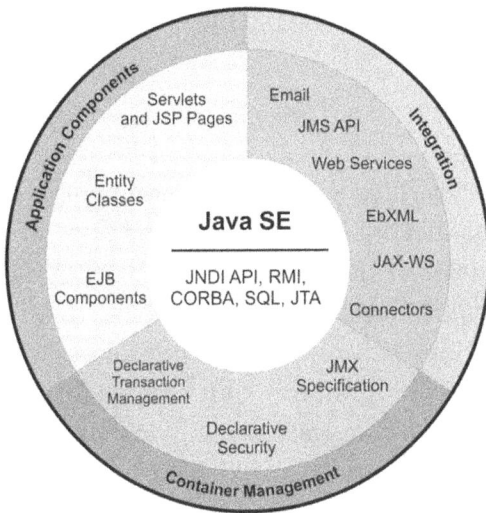

1.3 JDK vs. JRE

The JDK, or the Java Development Kit, is the application that all Java Developers should install on their machine. It contains the Java Compiler, Java-Doc creator, utility software, profilers, and your Java Runtime Environment (JRE).

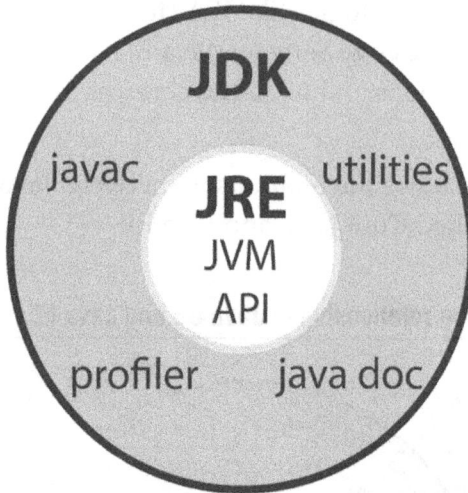

Figure 1.8 The Relationship of JDK and JRE

The JRE, or the Java Runtime Environment, is the
interpreter that needs to be installed by a Java Technology
Application user. As the word implies, it contains the
essential core libraries and other components. It also
contains your Java Virtual Machine interfaces(JVM) and
your Application Programming Interfaces (API). It is the
bare minimum that a casual user may install to use and run
Java-based applications. It does not support development
but is sufficient for executing compiled Java programs. The
following section takes a look at the JRE in detail.

1.4 The Java Runtime Environment (JRE)

The Java Runtime Environment contains two main
components:

1. The Java Virtual Machine (JVM) and the;
2. Application Program Interface (API)

In other programming languages, the API can be thought of as a set of pre-created code or libraries that allow programmers or developers to reuse and extend its capabilities.

Every time you run an application, you are executing the Java Runtime Environment. This means you are actually launching the JVM on top of the Operating System so that your valid `*.class` can now be interpreted. Your API, on the other hand, provides all the standard libraries that your program needs during runtime. The manner of accessing this standard API is the same across all platforms.

Before downloading your JRE, you need to first know what type of operating system you are using. There is a unique JRE for each operating system, but the implementation of the API for these JREs is the same.

1.4.1 The Java Virtual Machine (JVM)

As the name implies, the Java Virtual Machine is a Virtual Machine that is used to read Java bytecode. This Virtual Machine sits on top of the operating system and interprets compiled Java applications.

The Java Virtual Machine, also known as the JVM, can read compiled byte code, which is embedded inside your `*.class` file or `*.jar` file (JAR, short for Java archive). Your Java byte code ensures that the `*.class` that you're running came from a valid compilation process.

The JVM can also be customized. Certain companies would prefer to customize their own JVM; this is allowed by the Oracle software as long as the implementation of this JVM can run any valid `*.class` file and is approved by the Oracle software.

The compiler is checking the majority of the object's type, but there are still some parts of the code that should be checked during runtime. This enables the dynamism of Java, being able to check and evaluate forms and types during runtime.

The JVM can be executed on multiple operating environments. You just need to download the correct Java Runtime Environment (JRE) for your operating system.

1.5 The Garbage Collector

Garbage collection is the process of deallocating memory spaces that are no longer needed by your program during runtime. In some other programming languages, writing code for memory deallocation is the job of the programmer.

Garbage collection or memory deallocation, is the job of the Garbage Collector. The Garbage Collector (GC) is a system-level thread that runs in the background all the time the JRE is up and running. The GC tracks and monitors created objects in memory; if the object is dereferenced or is not used any longer, it is now ready for garbage collection. With the go signal of the Operating System, the GC runs and clears up the memory space that the object occupies, thus freeing up resources that other objects can use later on.

Figure 1.9 The Garbage Collector (GC)

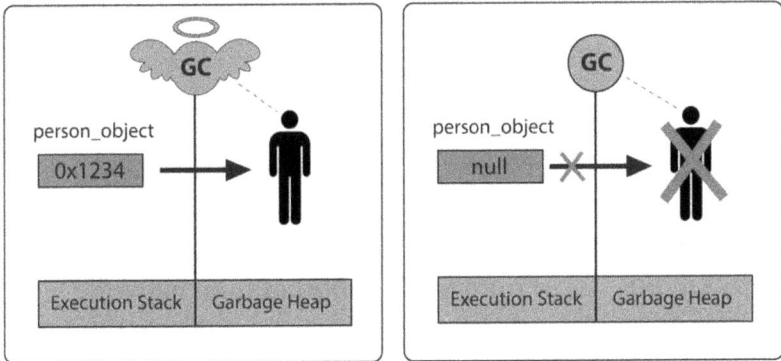

The implementation of the GC varies on different platforms. Since it is a system-level thread, the thread scheduler of the Operating System decides when the GC should run. Although you can set the GC in a runnable state by executing the method `System.gc();` this method call does not force the GC to run, it just puts it in a runnable (ready to run) state.

The runnable state is the state of the thread that is "ready" to run; it does not mean that it is actually running.

1.6 Three Tasks Performed By Java in Handling Code Security

Java ensures code security with three key steps.

1. **Class loading:** Only loads code from trusted sources to prevent unauthorized or harmful code from running

2. **Bytecode verification:** Checks the code for any violations or errors that could cause security risks.

3. **Interpretation:** The interpreter safely runs the code by managing it in a controlled environment, preventing harmful actions on the system.

1.6.1 Class Loading

The Class Loader loads all classes needed for the application to run. It also adds security by separating the name spaces for the classes of the local file system (FAT, UFS, NTFS, ZFS) from those imported from network resources. The Java Runtime Environment does not need to know about files and file systems because of the class loader. This limits any malicious software or scripts from penetrating your machine because local classes are always loaded first. After all the classes have been loaded, the memory layout comes after, during runtime.

1.6.2 Bytecode Verification

Your Java source file (*.java), once compiled, will produce a class file (*.class) which contains your Java bytecode.

The JVM lets your class file pass through a bytecode verifier to ensure that your compiled Java code is in accordance with the JVM specification that was set by the Oracle software. It also ensures that your class file is an actual product of a valid Java compilation.

The bytecode verifier ensures that your code adheres to the JVM specification and does not violate the system integrity by checking common programming errors that often lead to unpredictable behavior or sometimes data corruption. Some of these behaviors that are being checked by the bytecode verifier are array limits, use of an uninitialized reference, and illegal data conversions that may happen in your code (e.g., pointer value to integer value and vice versa).

The JVM verifies all bytecodes before it is executed; this verification consists of three types of checks:

1. Variables are always initialized, and references are always of the correct type.
2. Conditions and control structures branch to valid statement locations.
3. Access to private or package private data and methods is controlled.

The first two checks take place primarily during the actual verification step that occurs when the class is loaded and made eligible for use, while the third check is done dynamically, when variables and methods of the loaded class are being accessed by another class.

1.6.3 Interpretation

After loading the local class into memory and verifying if it is a valid class file, the next step is to interpret the class file. Runtime occurs during the interpretation of a valid class file. It is during this time that a RuntimeException can occur if there are irregularities found at runtime. RuntimeException will be discussed in a separate chapter in *Java Essentials Volume 2: Object-Oriented Programming and Beyond*.

In this chapter, you explored the essential characteristics that define the Java programming language and make it a preferred choice for many developers around the world. You learned that Java is known for its platform independence, object-oriented approach, and automatic memory management. You also became familiar with the three core editions of Java—Java SE, Jakarta EE (formerly Java EE), and Java ME—which are designed to support everything from desktop applications to enterprise and mobile solutions. You now understand the distinction between the JDK, which includes development tools, and the JRE, which provides the runtime needed to execute Java applications. Additionally, you discovered the purpose of the Java Garbage Collector, which manages memory automatically, and learned how Java upholds security by verifying bytecode, controlling class loading, and providing a secure runtime environment. These foundational concepts set the stage for deeper exploration in the chapters to come.

Chapter Summary

- Java is a robust, platform-independent, object-oriented language used widely in modern software development.

- Java comes in three main editions: Java SE (Standard Edition), Jakarta EE, and Java ME (Micro Edition), each serving specific development needs.

- The Java Development Kit (JDK) provides tools for compiling and running Java code, while the Java Runtime Environment (JRE) contains the environment necessary to run Java programs.

- The Garbage Collector in Java automatically reclaims unused memory, allowing developers to focus more on application logic.

- Java enforces strong code security through features like bytecode verification, classloaders, and a secure execution environment (sandboxing).

Quiz

1. Which of the following is not a feature of Java?

   a. Platform-dependent
   b. Object-oriented
   c. Secure
   d. Robust

2. Which Java edition is typically used for building web and enterprise-level applications?

   a. Java SE
   b. Java ME
   c. Java EE
   d. Java FX

3. What is the main purpose of the Java Development Kit (JDK)?

   a. To browse Java documentation
   b. To run compiled Java programs only
   c. To develop, compile, and run Java applications
   d. To manage system drivers

4. What does the Java Runtime Environment (JRE) include?

   a. A text editor
   b. Compiler and debugger
   c. Only the Java Virtual Machine (JVM) and libraries needed to run Java programs
   d. Source code files

5. **Which Java component automatically reclaims memory from unused objects?**
   a. Bytecode Interpreter
   b. Garbage Collector
   c. ClassLoader
   d. JVM Loader

6. **What is one of the key responsibilities of the Java classloader?**
   a. Execute main method
   b. Encrypt data
   c. Load classes into memory during runtime
   d. Run the compiler

7. **Java achieves platform independence through the use of:**
   a. Source code sharing
   b. Native machine code
   c. Bytecode interpreted by the JVM
   d. Virtual folders

8. **What does the term "sandboxing" refer to in Java?**
   a. A data visualization technique
   b. A virtual space for compiling code
   c. A secure environment for running potentially unsafe code
   d. A method for memory allocation

9. Which of the following is a valid reason to use Java ME?

   a. Developing web servers
   b. Programming desktop GUIs
   c. Creating mobile or embedded device apps
   d. Building enterprise services

10. The .java file is compiled into:

    a. Executable (.exe)
    b. Bytecode (.class)
    c. HTML file
    d. Assembly code

Answers

1 – a	2 – c	3 – c	4 – c	5 – b
6 – c	7 – c	8 – c	9 – c	10 – b

Further Reflection

1. Why do you think Java's platform independence has made it one of the most widely used programming languages in the world today? Consider how this feature impacts software distribution, updates, and compatibility.

2. Of the three Java editions (SE, EE, ME), which one do you see yourself using the most in your future projects, and why? Reflect on the kinds of applications you are interested in developing.

3. In what ways does automatic memory management through the Garbage Collector simplify programming for beginners and professionals alike? Think about how this affects your focus when writing and testing code.

4. How does the distinction between the JDK and the JRE help you understand the roles of development versus execution in Java? Consider your workflow as a programmer and where each tool fits in.

5. What are some real-world situations where Java's built-in security features (like classloaders, bytecode verification, and sandboxing) could be especially important? Explore examples like web applications, banking software, or mobile apps.

CHAPTER 2

Writing Your First Java Program

Key Learning Objectives

- Write and run your first Java program that displays a simple message on the screen.
- Use the `System.out.print()` and `System.out.println()` statements to print text output.
- Combine words and values using the + operator for text concatenation.
- Add special formatting to your output using escape sequence operators like `'\n'` for a new line and `'\t'` for a tab space.
- Understand and fix common compile-time and runtime errors that beginners often encounter.
- Explore and practice Java code using `JShell`, Java's interactive tool for testing code quickly.
- Learn basic Java syntax rules such as semicolons, case sensitivity, and the structure of a Java class.

Welcome to your first steps in learning Java! In this chapter, you'll learn how to write and run a basic Java program that displays text on the screen. You'll be introduced to the `System.out.print()` and `System.out.println()` statements, which is the standard way to show output in Java. You'll also discover how to combine text and variables using the + operator, and how to format your output using escape characters like `'\n'` for new lines and `'\t'` for tab spaces. Along the way, you'll learn how to recognize and fix common errors that can occur during compilation or execution.

Finally, you'll get hands-on experience with JShell, an interactive Java tool that lets you quickly try out code and see what it does. By the end of this chapter, you'll be ready to write simple Java programs with confidence.

2.1 "HelloWorld": Your First Java Application

Welcome to your first hands-on Java experience! In this section, you'll learn how to create a simple program called `HelloWorld.java`. This program displays the text "Hello, World" in the console. You'll use a basic text editor and the terminal to write, save, compile, and execute your code. To begin, open a basic text editor and type your first Java program.

```
1    // Filename: HelloWorld.java
2    public class HelloWorld {
3        public static void main(String[] args) {
4            System.out.println("Hello, World");
5        }
6    }
```

This program will be saved as `HelloWorld.java`, and its purpose is to display a simple message on the screen. In Java, every application begins with a `class` definition. For our example, we declare a class named `HelloWorld` using the line `public class HelloWorld` in line 2. Inside this class, we define the entry point of our program, which is the `main` method. The correct form of this method is `public static void main(String[] args)` in line 3, and it must be written exactly as shown, since Java is case-sensitive.

Here's a breakdown of Line 3: **public static void main(String[] args)**

- **public** means that your method is accessible anywhere.

- **static** is a type of modifier that means that your method will not be owned by a particular instance of the class, but the exclusive ownership will belong to the class.

- **void** is the return type of the main method. It means that the main method should not return any type of value.

- **main** is the name of the method. However, the main method is a special type of method that tells Java that this is the starting point of your application. All Java applications start their execution at the main method, and its method signature should be **public static void main(String[] args)**.

- **String[] args,** this goes inside the parameter list of your `main` method. This means that your `main` method should accept an array of `String` objects as its parameter. This can also be rewritten as **String args[],** essentially, both forms are the same.

Within the `main` method, we include a statement that prints text to the console using `System.out.println("Hello, World");` in line 4. This line instructs the Java runtime to display the words `"Hello, World"` exactly as written. Every statement in Java ends with a semicolon, so be sure to include it. With this, you now have a complete Java program, ready to be saved, compiled, and executed.

RULES

1. *Your public class name should have the same name as your filename.*

2. *There can only be one public class inside your .java file* Also, a pair of braces { } represents a scope. It is used to group related program segments. It can be used for control structures, methods, and classes.

3. *In your Java code, there should be an equal number of begin braces ({) and end braces (}).*

4. *The execution of any Java Application always starts with your main method. The signature of your main method should be:*

```
public static void main(String[] args)
```

5. *Everything in Java is Case-Sensitive*

Java is a case-sensitive language, meaning that identifiers such as `Main`, `main`, and `MAIN` are considered completely different. This applies to class names, method names, and variable names. Therefore, it's crucial that your file name matches the class name exactly, including uppercase and lowercase letters. For example, if your class is declared as `public class HelloWorld`, then the file name must be `HelloWorld.java`. If the capitalization does not match, the compiler will generate an error indicating that the `public class` must be declared in a file with the corresponding name. Additionally, Java programs require correct syntax. Statements must end with semicolons, and quotation marks, parentheses, and curly braces must always come in pairs. Failure to follow these basic rules will result in syntax errors during compilation.

2.1.1 Saving Your Program

Once you've written your program, the next step is to save it correctly. It's best practice to create a dedicated folder to organize your Java source files. Using the terminal window (if you're using a Mac machine or a Linux machine) or the Command Prompt (if you are using any Windows Machine), you can create a folder named `javacodes` by typing `mkdir javacodes`, and then change into that directory with the `cd javacodes` command.

Figure 2.1 Screenshot of the terminal Window in a Mac OS Machine

```
lawrence@Lawrences-MacBook-Air ~ % mkdir javacodes
lawrence@Lawrences-MacBook-Air ~ % cd javacodes
lawrence@Lawrences-MacBook-Air javacodes %
```

After that, return to your text editor and save your Java file within this folder. Make sure the file name matches the class name exactly and ends with a `.java` extension. In this case, since the class name is `HelloWorld`, the file must be named `HelloWorld.java`. Saving it with a different name or case will result in compilation errors. Once saved, you can verify the file's presence by listing the contents of the folder using the `ls` command (on the UNIX system or Mac OS) or `dir` on Windows.

Figure 2.2 Screenshot of the terminal window in a Mac OS Machine using the `ls` command

```
lawrence@Lawrences-MacBook-Air javacodes % ls
HelloWorld.java
lawrence@Lawrences-MacBook-Air javacodes %
```

To compile your Java source code, open your terminal and use the `javac` command, which stands for "Java compile." You need to provide the name of the file you want to compile, like so: `javac HelloWorld.java`. If your code is syntactically correct and matches the file name and class name, this command will produce a file named `HelloWorld.class`. This new file contains Java bytecode, which is the intermediate form of your program that the Java Virtual Machine (JVM) can execute. You can also list the folder contents again to verify that the `.class` file was successfully generated.

Figure 2.3	Screenshot of the terminal window in a Mac OS Machine after using `javac` to compile and the `ls` command to display the contents of the folder

```
● ● ●                    javacodes — -zsh — 77×9
lawrence@Lawrences-MacBook-Air javacodes % javac HelloWorld.java
lawrence@Lawrences-MacBook-Air javacodes % ls
HelloWorld.class        HelloWorld.java
lawrence@Lawrences-MacBook-Air javacodes %
```

After compiling, you're now ready to run your program. This time, use the `java` command followed by the name of the class that contains the main method, without adding the `.class` or `.java` extension. In our case, type `java HelloWorld`. If everything was done correctly, the console will display the message "`Hello, World`", confirming that your Java program has been successfully written, compiled, and executed.

For a Windows Machine, instead of opening the terminal window, we open the Command Prompt then we can also use the `mkdir` and the `cd` commands. But for the `ls`, we use dir instead for displaying the contents of the drive.

Figure 2.4 Screenshot of the terminal window in a Mac OS Machine running your first Java Program – `HelloWorld`.

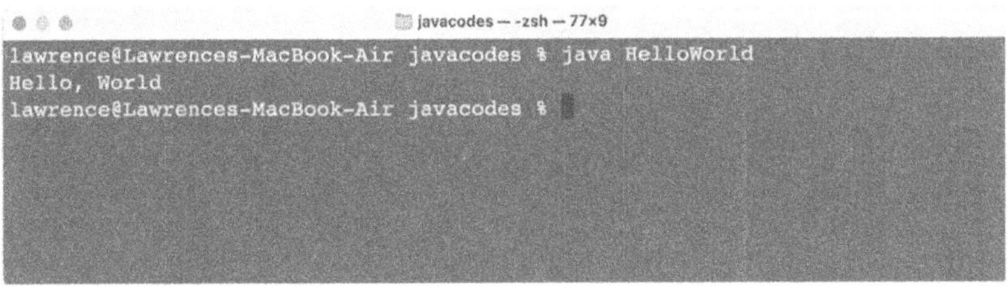

```
javacodes — -zsh — 77×9
lawrence@Lawrences-MacBook-Air javacodes % java HelloWorld
Hello, World
lawrence@Lawrences-MacBook-Air javacodes %
```

Congratulations—you have just created your first Java application!

2.2 The `System.out.println()` Method

To print an output, we can use the `System.out.println()` method to print something to the screen with the next line character ('\n') at the end. If you do not want the next line character included, you can use the `System.out.print()` method to print your output, and the cursor will be placed on the same line.

The ('+') operator is considered to be an overloaded operator, which means it can have different functions. It can be used for addition if both operands are numeric, and it can be used as a concatenation symbol if one of its operands is a `String`. A `String` is like a necklace made of letters, numbers, and symbols all tied together in a line.

The `System.out.println()` method statements in Table 2.1 will demonstrate how to display an output and the use of the plus ('+') operator.

Table 2.1 `System.out.println()` method statements

Java Statement	Output
System.out.println("Hello World");	Hello World
System.out.println("Hello\tWorld");	Hello World
System.out.println("Hello" + "\t" + "World");	Hello World
System.out.println("Hello\nWorld");	Hello World
System.out.print ("Hello World");	Hello World_
System.out.print ("Hello World\n");	Hello World _
System.out.print ("Hello World" + "\n");	Hello World _
int x = 100;	
System.out.println("x");	x
System.out.println(x);	100
System.out.println("x = " + x);	x = 100
System.out.println("5" + "10");	510
System.out.println(5 + 10);	15
System.out.println(5 + 10 + "abc");	15abc
System.out.println("abc" + 5 + 10);	abc510
System.out.println("abc" + (5 + 10));	abc15

2.3 Debugging Compile-Time Errors and Runtime Errors

Compile-time errors happen when there is a mistake in the code that stops it from being successfully compiled, like missing semicolons or incorrect syntax. Runtime errors occur after the program is successfully compiled but crash or behave unexpectedly when it is running, such as an integer number dividing by zero or accessing an invalid array location.

2.3.1 Common Compile-Time Errors

This section discusses the common compile-time errors encountered by those who are just starting out. Consider this sample compilation error:

```
HelloWorld.java:5: cannot resolve symbol
symbol : method printl (java.lang.String)
location: class java.io.PrintStream
System.out.printl("Hello, Java World");
                ^
```

The `println()` method is typed incorrectly.

The following are ways in which you can get such compile-time errors:

1. **Class and file naming:** Your Java source file should have the same name as your `public` class. If this rule is not followed correctly, you will have a compiler error similar to this:

```
TestHelloWord.java:7: public class
TestHelloWorld must be defined in a file called
"TestHelloWorld.java"
```

2. **Number of public classes in a Java source file:** You can only have one public class in a Java source file. If you declare more than one `public`, top-level class, you will have a similar compilation error. You can have many class declarations inside a Java source file as long as there is only one `class` that will be declared `public`, and the file name of the Java source file should be the same as the name of your `public` class.

Once you've encountered these compile-time errors, you need to edit your code, save it, and recompile. After fixing all the compile-time errors, you can now run your sample application.

The `javac` command is located under the subdirectory `\bin` of the installed Java Development Kit (JDK) directory. You must update your path directory and include the location of your `javac` executable file. If your `javac` command is not working, please refer back to Chapter 0.

2.3.2 Common Runtime Errors

After having a clean compile, it's now time for you to run your sample application. During runtime, you may encounter some errors. Here are some examples of common runtime errors:

1. **`Can't find class TestHelloWorld`**
   This runtime error will occur if you attempt to run a file that does not exist or if you are attempting to run a misspelled file. The filename should have the same spelling as the *filename*.class file.

2. **`Exception in thread "main" java.lang. NoSuchMethodError: main`**
   This means that your `main` method is incorrectly declared. Your `main` method must be `public`, and it should also be `static` and must have a return type of `void`, and it should also be called `main` and must accept an array of `String` objects as its parameter list.

   Another probable reason why this runtime error occurs is when you attempt to run a class file that does not have a `public static void main(String[] args)` method in it. The `main` method is the entry point of your application execution, thus, it should be present when you try to run your Java application.

Starting with Java 11 (JEP 330), the *"Launch Single-File Source-Code Programs"* feature was introduced. It allows direct execution of a Java source code file using the `java` launcher, without requiring explicit prior compilation with `javac`.

Instead of compiling your `.java` file into a `.class` file and then running the `.class` file, you can directly execute the `.java` file using the `java` command.

When you invoke `java` with a source file, the launcher automatically compiles the code in memory and then executes it. This avoids the creation of intermediate `.class` files on disk.

The requirement is that the source file must contain a top-level class with a `public static void main(String[] args)` method, which serves as the entry point for execution.

This command is now possible:

```
java HelloWorld.java
```

This will do an in-memory compilation and will run the source code directly without creating an external `.class` file.

Another cool feature was introduced in Java 21 called *"Simplified Entry Point"*. In earlier versions of Java, every program required a full class declaration and a specific main method signature:

```
public static void main(String[] args)
```

This method served as the standard entry point for any Java application and had to be placed inside a class. While this structure is powerful, it introduced a lot of boilerplate code—especially for beginners writing simple programs like `"Hello, World!"`.

Starting with Java 21, a new preview feature called `Unnamed Classes and Instance Main Methods` (introduced through `JEP 445`) allows you to write simpler Java programs without the need for an explicit class or the full static method declaration. For example:

```
1    void main() {
2        System.out.println("Hello, World!");
3    }
```

In this version, there is no `public`, no `static`, and no class name—just the logic. This greatly reduces complexity and helps new learners focus on programming concepts rather than language structure.

To compile and run this simplified version, preview features must be enabled using the `--enable-preview` flag during both compilation and execution:

To compile:

```
javac --enable-preview --release <jdkVer> HelloWorld.java
javac --enable-preview --release 21 HelloWorld.java
```

To run:

```
java --enable-preview HelloWorld
```

This enhancement in Java 21 (and expected in future versions in both JDK 23 and JDK 24) marks a significant step toward making Java more approachable, especially in educational settings and beginner-level development.

For newer JDK versions, it will be acceptable to just compile and run the code directly without the `--enable-preview --release 21` and `--enable-preview` options.

Here's a summary in table form.

Java Version	Code	Compile/Run Behavior
Java 8	Full class and static `main`	Must `javac` then `java`
Java 11	Same code	Can do `java HelloWorld.java`
Java 21	Just `void main()` in source	`java --enable-preview --source 21 HelloWorld.java`

2.4 Introduction to `JSHELL`

One of the most significant advancements in Java 9 is the introduction of `JShell`, a command-line tool designed to make the exploration of the language more interactive and immediate. Before `JShell`, running even the simplest Java code required setting up an entire class structure, followed by compilation and execution. This posed a barrier to quickly testing and experimenting with snippets of code or learning Java as a beginner. `JShell` changes this dynamic by loop-enabling a Read-Eval-Print-Loop (`REPL`) environment where users can directly execute Java code snippets and see the results instantly.

2.4.1 What is JShell?

`JShell` is a `REPL` (Read–Eval–Print Loop) tool introduced in Java 9 that allows developers to execute Java code interactively without needing to write a complete class or method structure. It provides a console where code can be typed, evaluated, and executed one statement or expression at a time. This makes `JShell` particularly useful for prototyping, debugging, and exploring Java code.

In essence, `JShell` is a tool that brings Java in line with the REPL tools available in many other programming languages like Python, Ruby, or Scala. Its primary goal is to facilitate quick experimentation, learning, and validation of small code fragments without the overhead of writing an entire Java application.

2.4.2 What is it For?

The primary purpose of `JShell` is to provide a streamlined environment where developers can quickly:

- **Test code snippets:** JShell is a great place to try out short code segments, whether you're exploring the behavior of a new API, testing an algorithm, or verifying language features.

- **Learn and teach Java:** JShell is an excellent tool for beginners to learn Java interactively. Instructors and learners can execute lines of code in real time, exploring the language with immediate feedback.

- **Debug small portions of code:** Instead of embedding debug print statements in full applications, developers can test smaller pieces of logic directly in JShell.

- **Prototype:** JShell is useful for rapidly prototyping small pieces of functionality without the overhead of creating a full project.

JShell's REPL nature eliminates the need for writing boilerplate code, compiling, and running a program. It helps you focus on the core logic, encouraging experimentation and learning.

2.4.3 How to Use JShell

Starting JShell is straightforward. After installing JDK 9 or later, simply open a terminal or command prompt and type: jshell <ENTER>

Figure 2.5 Jshell sample usage

```
lawrence — java • jshell — 83×9

lawrence@Lawrences-MacBook-Air ~ % jshell
|  Welcome to JShell -- Version 16.0.2
|  For an introduction type: /help intro

jshell>
```

This command launches the JShell environment, and you will be greeted with a prompt (jshell>) where you can start entering Java code.

For example, to perform a simple arithmetic operation, you can type:

```
5 + 10 <ENTER>
```

Figure 2.6 Jshell sample usage with expression evaluation

```
lawrence — java • jshell — 83x9

lawrence@Lawrences-MacBook-Air ~ % jshell
  Welcome to JShell -- Version 16.0.2
  For an introduction type: /help intro

jshell> 5 + 10
$1 ==> 15

jshell>
```

JShell immediately evaluates the expression and prints the result. Similarly, you can declare variables, write methods, or even define classes:

Figure 2.7 Jshell sample usage with method declaration and usage

```
lawrence — java • jshell — 84x14
jshell> int a = 10;
a ==> 10

jshell> String greet() {
   ...>      return "Hello, JShell!";
   ...> }
|  created method greet()

jshell> greet()
$4 ==> "Hello, JShell!"

jshell>
```

You can see that the method greet() is defined and invoked immediately, without having to compile a class or create a main method.

JShell can also import classes and libraries as needed, so you can explore third-party libraries interactively. For instance, you can easily import utility classes like the `java.util.Scanner` or your own classes from other packages using JShell.

To exit JShell, you have to type /ex in the Jshell prompt. From there, you will get a Goodbye message from JShell, and you will go back to your OS prompt.

Figure 2.8 **Exiting Jshell**

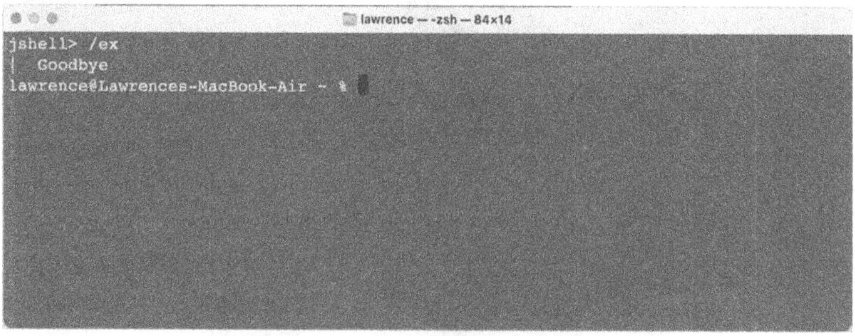

By now, you've written your first Java program, learned how to save it properly, compiled it using the `javac` command, and executed it with the `java` command. Along the way, you've also learned how to identify and fix common errors, including both compilation and runtime issues. You've seen how important it is to match class names with file names, follow Java's strict syntax rules, and provide a properly formatted main method. You've also been introduced to the `System.out.print()` and `System.out.println()` statements for printing output. These foundational skills are essential for all Java programmers, and they will continue to serve you well as you progress to more advanced topics.

Chapter Summary

- When creating a Java source code, remember that the public class name SHOULD be the same as your filename.

- The plus (+) operator is an overloaded operator; it can be used for concatenation, or it can be used for addition depending on the type of operands surrounding it.

- Errors are a normal part of the life of a programmer. If a series of compilation errors are encountered, be sure to focus on the first error, debug it, then save your code and recompile. Always focus on the first compilation error because the succeeding ones are echo errors.

- `JShell` is a powerful addition to the Java ecosystem, particularly beneficial for developers and learners who want to explore the language interactively. By eliminating the initial setup and boilerplate code, `JShell` allows you to focus on understanding and experimenting with Java concepts. Whether you're testing a small snippet of code, debugging a specific logic, or teaching Java to a new audience, `JShell` makes the process much smoother and more intuitive.

Quiz

1. **Which of the following statements is NOT TRUE?**

   a. The javac (Java Compiler) is a part of the Java Runtime Environment

   b. The Java Runtime Environment is a piece of software you install to let the user run Java-based applications

   c. The Java Virtual Machine is a part of the Java Runtime Environment.

   d. The Java Development Kit is the piece of software you need to install to enable the user to write and run Java-based applications.

2. **Given the class declaration below:**

```
public class MyFirstJavaProgram {

    public static void main() {

        System.out.println("Will I run?");
    }
}
```

   Which of the following statements is TRUE?

   a. The code will compile and will run with an output of: Will I run?

   b. The code will NOT compile

   c. The code will compile, but will NOT run.

   d. The code will compile and run with no output.

3. Given the class declaration below:

```
public class MyFirstJavaProgram {

    public static void main(String[] args) {

        int a = 10, b = 20;
        // insert code here
    }
}
```

Which of the following codes below will NOT cause the program to print the output: a = 10, b = 20

a. `System.out.print ("a = 10" , "b = 20");`
b. `System.out.print ("a = " + a + ", b = " + b);`
c. `System.out.print ("a = " + 10 + ", b = " + 20);`
d. `System.out.print ("a = 10, b = 20");`

4. Take a look at the snippet below:

```
System.out.print("Java");
System.out.print("Programming");
System.out.print("is");
System.out.print("Fun");
```

Assuming the snippet is inside a valid Java code, what will be the output?

a. Java is Fun
b. Java Programming is Fun
c. JavaProgrammingisFun
d. Java
   Programming
   is
   Fun

5. **What should you do with the errors that you encounter during compile time?**

   a. Debug ALL errors immediately so that you can save time.

   b. You can ignore these errors; they will eventually go away.

   c. Randomly guess the solution to these errors and hope that you get them right.

   d. Debug the first error first, then save your code, then recompile and debug the other errors if there are still any left.

6. **What gets printed?**

```
System.out.println(5 + 10 + "xyz");
```

   a. 510xyz
   b. 15xyz
   c. Nothing gets printed; this will cause a compilation error.
   d. Nothing gets printed; this will cause a runtime error.

7. **Why will the statement below cause a compilation error?**

```
System.out.println("Will I be printed?');
```

a. The code will compile and run and will print: Will I be printed?

b. The code will cause a compilation error because the String literal is unclosed; there's a missing double-quote (")

c. The code will cause a compilation error because the String literal is unclosed; there's a missing single-quote (')

d. The code will compile but will NOT run because of a runtime error.

8. **Which of the following statements IS NOT TRUE about the ('+') operator?**

a. The ('+') operator is an overloaded operator; it can be used for addition and concatenation of values.

b. If the operands are both numeric, the '+' operator functions as an addition operator.

c. If the operands are both boolean, the '+' operator will put both boolean values side by side.

d. If the operands are both String values, the '+' operator will concatenate both values.

9. **Given the code below:**

```
class MyClass {

    public static void main(String args[]) {

        System.out.println("I love coding...");
    }
}
```

The code was saved as `Hello.java`
Which of the following statements is TRUE?

a. The Java source code Hello.java will compile and will produce a class file named MyClass.class

b. The code will not compile because the class name is not the same as the file name.

c. The code will not compile because of the incorrect parameter of the main method; the parameter should be String[] args and not String args[]

d. The code will not compile because there are missing comments in the Java source code.

10. **Which of the following statements IS NOT TRUE?**

a. The number of begin curly braces '{' should always have the same number of end curly braces '}'

b. In a Java Source code, you are allowed to have multiple classes, but only one public class is allowed.

c. The public class in a Java Source code must match its filename.

d. All Java source code MUST have a public class.

Answers
---

1 – a	2 – c	3 – a	4 – c	5 – d
6 – b	7 – b	8 – c	9 – a	10 – d

Coding Tasks

Coding Problem 1:

Create two Java Programs named `TriangleVer1.java` and `TriangleVer2.java`.

Both codes should display the same output, a triangle having four layers of asterisks:

```
   *
  ***
 *****
*******
```

For `TriangleVer1.java` you can use several `System.out.println()` methods.

But for `TriangleVer2.java` try to use only one (1) `System.out.println()` method.

Explore the use of `'\n'`, `'\t'`, and spaces to format your triangle.

Coding Problem 2:

Write a Java program named `HelloFormatted.java` that prints the following message to the console using only one `System.out.println()` with `'\t'` (tab) and `'\n'` (newline) escape characters:

Expected Output:

```
Hello, World!
Welcome to Java Programming.
This is your first Java class.
```

Coding Problem 3:

The following code contains three errors. Rewrite the program so that it compiles and runs successfully, displaying the intended output. Name the class `FixMe.java`.

Here's the code with the error:

```
public class fixme {
        public static void main(string[] args)
        System.out.println("I'm fixed, yey!");
}
```

Expected Output:

```
I'm fixed, yey!
```

Practice More, Get Better!

Additional coding tasks for this chapter are available in the exclusive online resources that accompany this book.

CHAPTER 3
User Input, Identifiers, Keywords, and The Primitive Data Types

Key Learning Objectives

- The three types of Java comments
- Semicolons, blocks, and white spaces
- Java identifiers and keywords
- Java programming language coding conventions
- The primitive data types
- The `Math` class and `Scanner` class

In this chapter, we will dive into the foundational elements of Java syntax and structures that are essential for writing clear and efficient code. Understanding how to accept user inputs using the `Scanner` class and the various forms of Java comments within your code will help improve readability and maintenance. We will also explore the significance of proper coding and naming conventions, which contribute to the overall quality of your programming practices. Additionally, you'll gain insight into the primitive data types available in Java, enabling you to choose the most appropriate type for your variables and operations. Finally, we will touch upon the built-in methods of the `Math` class provided by Java's standard library, which can enhance your mathematical computations and overall programming experience.

3.1 Three Types of Java Comments

Now, let's talk about comments in Java. Comments are used to put a message for your future self or for your other teammates so that you don't have to retrace your code every time you go back to it after a few days, a few months, or a few years. In the Java programming language, we have three types of comments. We have the single-line comment, the multi-line comment, and the Java documentation comments.

1. **Single line comment:** The single line comment is used to comment out a single line of code. You start it off with a pair of forward slash symbols. Any and all texts found after the double slash are considered comments.

```
// Single Line Comment
```

2. **Multi-line comment:** We also have the multi-line comment. Multi-line comments are used to comment out multiple lines of code. You start it off with a slash (/) followed by an asterisk (*) symbol, and then you terminate it or end it with an asterisk (*) followed by a forward slash (/).

```
/*
Multi Line Comment
*/
```

All texts that you find inside these multi-line comments are considered comments. Let's say you have a piece of code that you would like to remove for testing purposes; you do not need to delete it immediately. Instead, you just need to surround it with a multi-line comment so that when you want your code back, you simply remove the comments surrounding it and do not end up retyping the code block again.

3. **Java documentation comments:** Java documentation comments, also known as javadoc comments, are used to document or to put Java documentation in your source code. Here's how to write Javadoc comments:

```
/**
Java Documentation Comment
*/
```

This type of comment is used to provide descriptions of what the structure is all about. It is normally placed on top of a class declaration, an attribute declaration, or a method declaration so as to provide a description of what the said construct can do. After coding the application and putting in the proper Javadoc comments, you can now create an HTML file that is very similar to the Java API Documentation that can be launched and viewed on your browser.

The Java 23 API Documentation can be accessed through this link: https://docs.oracle.com/en/java/javase/23/docs/api/index.html. (Link also provided in the online resources section of this book.) You can then create your own Java Documentation in any IDE, such as the NetBeans IDE. Here's a sample screenshot of a Project in NetBeans:

Figure 3.1 shows a sample NetBeans project named JavaDocSampleProj with two packages named `model` and `test`. `Person.java` is placed under the package `model`, while the class `TestPerson.java` is placed under the package `test`. Both source codes contain JavaDoc comments describing the class and the methods.

Figure 3.1 Screenshot of a NetBeans Project

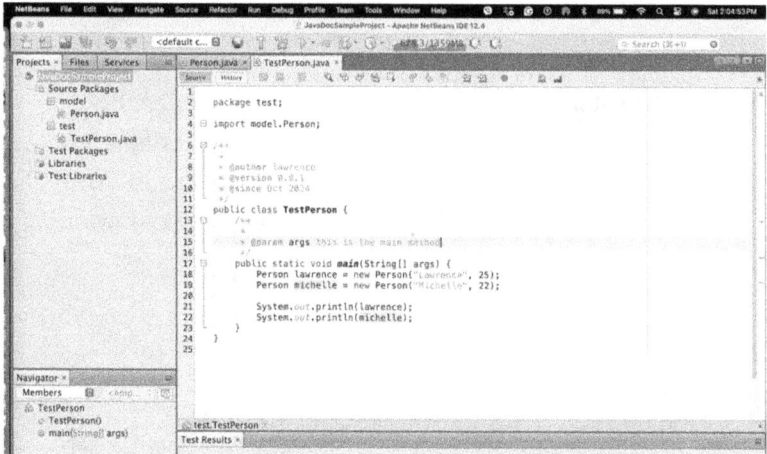

Figure 3.2 shows how to generate the Java Documentation Comment in NetBeans IDE by right-clicking on the Project and choosing the Generate Javadoc option from the list of choices. This will let the NetBeans IDE go through all the Java source code, read all the Javadoc comments inside all the Java source code, and generate the HTML version of the Java Documentation for that project. Figure 3.3 shows the runtime of the Java Documentation of the JavaDocSampleProject generated by NetBeans.

Figure 3.2 Screenshot of a NetBeans Project to generate the Java documentation of the Active Project

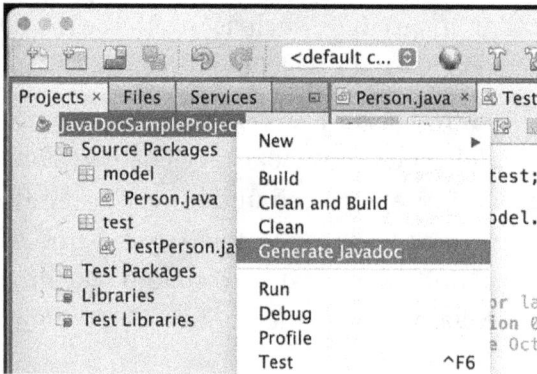

Figure 3.3 Screenshot of a Google Chrome browser showing the generated JavaDoc of the existing Project

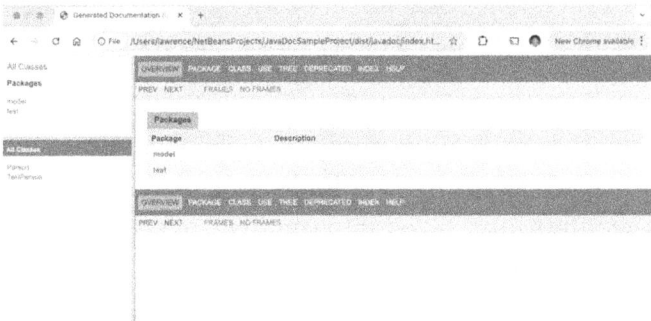

In some IDEs, there is a feature that will help you generate the Java documentation by choosing an option called "Generate Java-Doc". The Java documentation can be generated in most IDEs, including NetBeans, Eclipse, and IntelliJ.

We can also do the same feature via command line without the use of any IDE. Java provides a built-in tool called `javadoc` that can be used to generate HTML documentation from Java source files containing special comments known as Javadoc comments. These comments begin with /** and are commonly used to describe classes, methods, constructors, and fields in a format that can be automatically extracted and formatted.

The basic command (all JDK versions) to generate documentation from a valid Java source file, use the following command in your terminal or command prompt:

```
javadoc MyClass.java
```

This command will produce a set of HTML files in the current directory under a `doc` folder (or wherever the output is directed), representing the public API of `MyClass.java` as documented by the Javadoc comments.

To specify an output directory explicitly, use:

```
javadoc -d docs MyClass.java
```

This will generate the documentation in a folder named docs.

For most use cases, the `javadoc` command remains consistent across different versions of the JDK. However, there are some key considerations when working with newer features introduced in recent JDK releases, especially preview features like unnamed classes.

Here's a summarized table showing the key differences and considerations:

Feature / Scenario	Traditional JDK (e.g., JDK 8–17)	Newer JDK (e.g., JDK 21+)
Standard class with Javadoc comments	Supported	Supported
Use of preview features	Not supported	Requires `--enable-preview` flag
Modules and advanced structures	Limited support	Better support with `--module-path`, etc.
Unnamed classes	Not recognized	Not currently recognized by `javadoc`

As of now, preview features like *unnamed classes* are not fully supported by the javadoc tool, even in JDK 21+. Therefore, when working with these new Java source formats, it is recommended to keep your API-documentable code in traditional, named classes if you intend to generate Javadoc from them.

If your code uses modules (introduced in Java 9), you can also include module-specific flags such as:

```
javadoc --module-path mods -d docs my.module.name
```

3.2 Semicolons, Blocks, and White Spaces

1. **Semicolon:** A semicolon is used by Java as a language signal that it is at the end of a statement. Deleting a

semicolon will tell the Java compiler that the next line of your code is a continuation of the current line. This is a common rule for programming languages like C, C++, and Java. Other programming languages don't require semicolons like Python, Ruby, or Visual Basic. So, if you have a programming background using a different programming language, be sure to include a semicolon in Java if you want to end a statement.

```
int x = a + b
          + c + d;
```

is the same as:

```
int x = a + b + c + d;
```

2. **Blocks:** A block, also known as a scope, is used to group related statements together. We use curly braces to represent a block ({ }). Curly braces are normally used on classes, methods, and control structures like if-else, while loop, for loop, etc.
Having a block also signifies the scope of the variable. Consider the following program snippet:

```
10  public void doSomething() {
11
12      int x;
13
14      if (true) {
15
16              int x;   // compilation error,
                         // duplicate variable
17      }
18  }
```

The given code snippet will have a compilation error on line 16 for having a duplicate declaration of the variable x that was declared in line 12. You can only declare a variable once inside a specific scope of code.

The variable x declared in line 12 is inside the scope
of the method doSomething(), so declaring another
variable x in line 16 creates a duplicate variable
declaration of the said variable x.

But if we rewrite it this way:

```
10   public void doSomething() {
11
12        // int x;
13
14        if (true) {
15
16                int x;   // compilation ok!,
                           // no duplicate variable
17        }
18        int x;
19   }
```

The compilation of this sample code snippet will be ok.
The first variable x, declared in line 16, will only have a
life span within the **if** curly braces, between lines 14 to
17, and it will be destroyed after line 17. Therefore, the
variable x declared on line 18 is valid, as it is treated as
a new declaration with no duplication.

3. **White spaces:** These are the spaces, tabs, and enter keys
(or next line characters) in your code. Java ignores
white spaces, which means any amount of white space
in Java is allowed. White spaces are normally used for
formatting so that your code can be readable in the eyes
of a casual reader. For example, the given sample code:

```
for (int i = 0; i < 3; i++) { System.out.println(i); }
```

is the same as:

```
for (int i = 0; i < 3; i++) {

        System.out.println(i);

}
```

Both codes are the same, but neither of them is pleasing to the eye. The first one occupied a single line of code. It can work, but your co-workers, teammates, or anybody who sees your code will not appreciate the way you wrote it.

The second version is better. It uses tabs and spaces that make the code more readable because you can immediately identify the pairing of the begin and end curly braces and the code inside them.

3.3 Java Identifiers

Identifiers are used to "identify" something. We use names or identifiers to *identify* variables, methods, classes, constant values, file names, and other coding elements. Think of it as a label that helps the programmer and the computer refer to specific parts of a program. Essentially, they serve as the customizable names we assign to various components to make the code readable and logical.

Creating identifiers in Java requires following specific rules to ensure they are valid and recognizable by the compiler. These rules include:

1. **Start with a letter or underscore:** Identifiers must begin with a letter (A-Z or a-z), an underscore (_), or a dollar sign ($). They cannot start with a digit.

2. **Use only allowed characters:** Identifiers can contain letters, digits (0-9), underscores, and dollar signs, but no spaces or special symbols like '@', '#', or '!'.

3. **Avoid reserved keywords:** Words that Java reserves as keywords, like `int` or `class`, cannot be used as identifiers.

4. **Account for case sensitivity:** Java identifiers are case-sensitive, so `MyVar` and `myvar` would be treated as two different identifiers.

5. **No length limit:** While Java does not impose a specific length limit, identifiers should be concise yet descriptive

for better readability. These rules ensure identifiers are both functional and meaningful within the code.
Here are valid examples of Java identifiers:

```
Int, $$$, ___, basic_pay, OverTime, getTaxPayer,
thisIsAVeryLoooooongVariableName
```

Here are examples of invalid Java identifiers:

```
int, 123, ---, gross-Pay, over time pay
```

For best practices, while not enforced by the compiler, the following conventions are widely adopted in professional Java development:

- Class names: PascalCase (e.g., StudentInfo)
- Method and variable names: camelCase (e.g., calculateSum, studentAge)
- Constants: UPPER_CASE_WITH_UNDERSCORES (e.g., MAX_VALUE)
- Avoid using $ or _ unless specifically required (e.g., generated code or legacy codebases)

3.4 The Java Keywords

The Java keywords are special reserved words that have predefined meanings and purposes in the language. They form the core syntax and structure of Java programs, guiding how the code is written and interpreted. Keywords cannot be used as names for variables, methods, or other identifiers because they are essential for Java to recognize specific instructions. These words enable developers to perform tasks like creating loops, defining classes, or handling data types while ensuring that Java code is consistent and follows its design principles. Table 3.1 shows the list of Java keywords including new keywords and reserved identifiers added in later versions.

Table 3.1   List of Java Keywords Reference Chart (Java 8 to Java 23)

	Keyword	Java 8	Java 9	Java 10	Java 14	Java 16	Java 17	Java 21	Notes
1	abstract	sk	sk	sk	sk	sk	sk	sk	Class modifier
2	assert	sk	sk	sk	sk	sk	sk	sk	Debugging
3	boolean	sk	sk	sk	sk	sk	sk	sk	Primitive type
4	break	sk	sk	sk	sk	sk	sk	sk	Control flow
5	byte	sk	sk	sk	sk	sk	sk	sk	Primitive type
6	case	sk	sk	sk	sk	sk	sk	sk	Switch case
7	catch	sk	sk	sk	sk	sk	sk	sk	Exception handling
8	char	sk	sk	sk	sk	sk	sk	sk	Primitive type
9	class	sk	sk	sk	sk	sk	sk	sk	Class declaration
10	const	r	r	r	r	r	r	r	Reserved only
11	continue	sk	sk	sk	sk	sk	sk	sk	Loop control
12	default	sk	sk	sk	sk	sk	sk	sk	Interface/ switch
13	do	sk	sk	sk	sk	sk	sk	sk	Loop
14	double	sk	sk	sk	sk	sk	sk	sk	Primitive type
15	else	sk	sk	sk	sk	sk	sk	sk	Conditional
16	enum	sk	sk	sk	sk	sk	sk	sk	Enum type
17	extends	sk	sk	sk	sk	sk	sk	sk	Inheritance
18	final	sk	sk	sk	sk	sk	sk	sk	Constant/ modifier
19	finally	sk	sk	sk	sk	sk	sk	sk	Exception cleanup
20	float	sk	sk	sk	sk	sk	sk	sk	Primitive type
21	for	sk	sk	sk	sk	sk	sk	sk	Loop

	Keyword	Java 8	Java 9	Java 10	Java 14	Java 16	Java 17	Java 21	Notes
22	goto	r	r	r	r	r	r	r	Reserved only
23	if	sk	sk	sk	sk	sk	sk	sk	Conditional
24	implements	sk	sk	sk	sk	sk	sk	sk	Interfaces
25	import	sk	sk	sk	sk	sk	sk	sk	Package usage
26	instanceof	sk	sk	sk	sk	sk	sk	sk	Type check
27	int	sk	sk	sk	sk	sk	sk	sk	Primitive type
28	interface	sk	sk	sk	sk	sk	sk	sk	Interface
29	long	sk	sk	sk	sk	sk	sk	sk	Primitive type
30	native	sk	sk	sk	sk	sk	sk	sk	Native method
31	new	sk	sk	sk	sk	sk	sk	sk	Object creation
32	package	sk	sk	sk	sk	sk	sk	sk	Declaring packages
33	private	sk	sk	sk	sk	sk	sk	sk	Access control
34	protected	sk	sk	sk	sk	sk	sk	sk	Access control
35	public	sk	sk	sk	sk	sk	sk	sk	Access control
36	return	sk	sk	sk	sk	sk	sk	sk	Method return
37	short	sk	sk	sk	sk	sk	sk	sk	Primitive type
38	static	sk	sk	sk	sk	sk	sk	sk	Class member
39	strictfp	sk	sk	sk	sk	sk	sk	sk	Floating point
40	super	sk	sk	sk	sk	sk	sk	sk	Parent reference
41	switch	sk	sk	sk	sk	sk	sk	sk	Conditional
42	synchronized	sk	sk	sk	sk	sk	sk	sk	Thread control

	Keyword	Java 8	Java 9	Java 10	Java 14	Java 16	Java 17	Java 21	Notes
43	this	sk	sk	sk	sk	sk	sk	sk	Object reference
44	throw	sk	sk	sk	sk	sk	sk	sk	Throw exception
45	throws	sk	sk	sk	sk	sk	sk	sk	Exception declaration
46	transient	sk	sk	sk	sk	sk	sk	sk	Serialization
47	try	sk	sk	sk	sk	sk	sk	sk	Exception block
48	void	sk	sk	sk	sk	sk	sk	sk	Method return type
49	volatile	sk	sk	sk	sk	sk	sk	sk	Thread visibility
50	while	sk	sk	sk	sk	sk	sk	sk	Loop
51	var		p	sk	sk	sk	sk	sk	Restricted identifier
52	_		k	k	k	k	k	k	Reserved keyword
53	yield			k	sk	sk	sk	sk	Switch expression
54	record			p	k	sk	sk	Data class
55	sealed				p	k	sk	Sealed class
56	non-sealed				p	k	sk	Sealed class subtype
57	permits				p	k	sk	Allowed subclasses

Legend:

sk = Standard keyword
r = Reserved but not used
p = Introduced as a preview in earlier versions
k = Became reserved or a keyword in the version

As for null, true, and false, they are **NOT** Java keywords. They are "literal values".

Literal values are values that you can assign to a variable. A null value can be assigned to a reference data type variable, while `true` and `false` are possible values of a `boolean` variable.

3.4.1 Two Special Keywords

The keywords `const` and `goto` are considered "special keywords". These are Java keywords, but are not allowed to be used in coding. There are no implementations of these keywords in the Java Programming Language, but the Java creators decided to consider them as reserved keywords so that in future releases of Java or other similar technologies, `const` and `goto` may not be used anymore.

3.5 Java Programming Language Coding Conventions

3.5.1 Packages

Packages are normally written in small letters, and it is usually the reverse URL of your application. As we have discussed in the previous chapter, the package layout is usually your directory structure. Here's an example of a package:

```
com.myapp.domain;
```

3.5.2 Classes, `Interfaces`, and `enum` Types

As for classes, `interfaces`, and `enum` types, we normally use the CLC, or the *Capital-Lower-Capital* naming convention. The identifier name starts with a capital letter, followed by lowercase letters. If there is a succeeding word, then you capitalize the first letter of the succeeding word. Here are some examples of names of classes, interfaces, and `enum` types.

```
TestPerson, Flyer, BankAccount, MonthsOfTheYear
```

3.5.3 Methods and Variables

Example of method names:

```
getName(), setName(), addButton()
```

Example of variable names:

```
name, age, finalGrade
```

Methods and variables use the camelback naming convention. C/C++ developers normally use camelback as a way to write methods and variables alike. You start your identifier name with a small letter, and if you need to use another word, you capitalize the first letter of the succeeding word. A method should have a pair of parentheses at the end, and it may or may not include parameters inside the parentheses.

3.5.4 Constants

Examples of constants include:

```
STUDENT_NUMBER, SPEED_OF_LIGHT,
PI, PULL_OF_GRAVITY
```

Constants are declared in ALL CAPS. An identifier that is written in all capital letters normally represents a final variable, also known as a constant identifier. In the event that your constant identifier is composed of multiple words, you separate these words with an underscore (_) symbol.

Here's how we write them properly in Java using the final keyword:

```
final int STUDENT_NUMBER = 50;
final double SPEED_OF_LIGHT = 299792458; // in m/s
final double PI = 3.141592653589793;
final double PULL_OF_GRAVITY = 9.80665; // in m/s^2
```

3.5.5 Control Structures

```
for (int i = 0; i < 5; i++){
    // do something
}
```

Control Structures like `if-else`, `switch-case`, `do-while`, `while`, and `for-loop` are usually followed by a block or a scope that is enclosed in a pair of curly (`{}`) braces. We use white spaces such as tabs, spaces, and enter keys to make our control structure codes more readable. The actual discussion on these control structures will be discussed in Chapter 5.

3.5.6 Spacing and Indentations

As for the spacing of your code, we encourage using two to four spaces as an indentation if your code is inside a pair of curly braces. This way, at one glance, you will have an idea of which lines of code are inside the curly braces, which is normally called your code block. These spaces are used only for readability, as spaces are ignored by Java.

Also, we encourage using one statement per line, terminated by a semicolon (`;`). Semicolons are mandatory to end a Java statement. Having multiple statements in a single line, even if coded properly, can sometimes cause confusion at a glance. To avoid this, a single statement terminated by a semicolon per line is always the best way to go.

3.5.7 Comments

Putting the comments described in section 3.1 in your code is a good programming practice for documentation purposes. Both single-line and multi-line comments are beneficial to insert your human-formatted thoughts into your Java code.

On top of that, JavaDoc comments can do much more. After including all the descriptions you included in your code, and after the coding and testing processes, you can start building your documentation by harnessing the power of your IDE and choosing the option "Generate Java Doc" for the NetBeans IDE. This will automatically read the JavaDoc comments you placed inside your code and translate them into an HTML format that you can also send as technical documentation.

Following these conventions will allow you and your colleagues to work better by allowing you to write code that is readable and well-documented.

3.6 The Primitive Data Types

There are eight primitive data types. **Primitive data types** are the most basic types of data that represent simple values directly in memory. They are predefined by the language and are not objects. These types are the building blocks for data manipulation in Java. The eight primitive data types are as follows: `byte`, `short`, `int`, `long`, `float`, `double`, `char`, and `boolean`.

Data types that are not a part of the eight primitive data types are considered **reference data types**. In Java, reference data types are types that store references (or memory addresses) to the actual data rather than the data itself. They include objects, arrays, and interfaces. Unlike primitive data types that hold their values directly, reference types point to locations in memory where the data resides. More discussion about reference data types will be covered in *Java Essentials Volume 2: Object-Oriented Programming and Beyond*.

The eight primitive data types can be further classified as follows:

1. **Integral data types:** These contain whole number values and may have both negative and positive values, including zero (0). The following are types of integral data types:

a. byte – *an* 8-bit *data type, legal values may range between* -2^7 *to* $+2^7$ – 1 *or* -128 *to* +127

b. short – *a* 16-bit *data type, legal values may range between* -2^{15} *to* $+2^{15}$ – 1 *or* -32,768 *to* +32,767

c. int – *a* 32-bit *data type, legal values may range between* -2^{31} *to* $+2^{31}$ – 1 *or* -2,147,483,648 *to* 2,147,483,647

d. long – *a* 64-bit *data type, legal values may range between* -2^{63} *to* $+2^{63}$ – 1 *or* -9,223,372,036,854,775,808 *to* -9,223,372,036,854,775,807

Table 3.2	Memory sizes of integral data types	

Integer Length	Name or Type	Range
8 bits	byte	-2^7 to 2^7-1
16 bits	short	-2^{15} to 2^{15}-1
32 bits	int	-2^{31} to 2^{31}-1
64 bits	long	-2^{63} to 2^{63}-1

Among the four, int is the default integral data type. This means that if you see a whole number value without any declaration, either a negative or a positive value, it is safe to assume that it is an int.

The default number format is base 10 (decimal). For other number formats, the following syntax must be followed:

Base 10 - Decimal   - 9, 87, 0

Base 8   - Octal   - 077, -012

Base 16 - Hexadecimal - 0xABCD, -0x1234

Base 2   - Binary   - 0B0100_1110_0101_0011

> **Note**
>
> Java SE 7 and newer versions offers the following added features:
>
> - The underscore (_) can now be used as a part of the literal value of Java SE 7.
> - The binary (base 2) format was also introduced in Java SE 7. A binary value can be written by prefixing a series of binary numbers (1's and 0's) with 0B or 0b, like 0b0100.

2. **Floating Points:** As for fractional values, you have two data types. You have the float data type and the double.

   a. float – *32 bits*

      1.23f, -5.14F

   b. double – *64 bits*

      3.14, 5.10D, -0.012d, 1.23456e-2

Table 3.3   Memory sizes of floating-point data types

Float Length	Name or Type
32 bits	float
64 bits	double

The double data type is the default data type for fractional values, which means that if you see a fractional value that has no data type declaration, it is safe to assume that it is a double value. A double data type occupies 64 bits of memory space, while a float only occupies 32 bits of memory space. Either a capital 'F' or a small 'f' at the end of a fractional value must be included as a suffix.

Table 3.4 Sample of floating point values

3.1415	A simple floating-point value a double
6.82E23	A large floating-point value
2.718F	A simple float size value
123.4E+306D	A large double value with redundant D

A double value can also include a 'D' or 'd' as a suffix. Although it's not needed, it can still be placed there if you want to declare it for readability purposes only.

3. **Textual Type:** A textual data type is used to store a single 16-bit Unicode character, allowing it to represent a wide range of symbols, letters, and digits from various languages, not just the ASCII set.

   a. char – *16 bits*

   ```
   'a', '\t', '\u0061'
   ```

There are three ways to declare a character, but either way, a char must be inside a pair of single quotes. You can put any Unicode value, an escape sequence character, or a Unicode notation inside a pair of single quotes to represent a character value. The Unicode notation is prefixed with '\u' character followed by hexadecimal numbers.

Table 3.5 Sample Representation of char Values

'a'	The letter a
'\t'	The tab character
'\u????'	A specific Unicode character, ????, is replaced with exactly four hexadecimal digits. For example, '\u03A6' is the Greek letter phi [φ]

4. **Logical Type:** It is used to represent true or false values. This type is essential for making decisions in a program, especially in conditions and control structures.

   a. boolean

   A boolean primitive data type can only have two possible values; it can either have a true or a false value. A common mistake by newbies, especially if they have a C programming background, is that they think that a boolean data type has a numeric equivalent.

   Take a look at this snippet:

```
boolean doorIsOpen = false;
// I want to open the door,
doorIsOpen++;        // incompatible types
```

   You cannot increment the value of doorIsOpen by one. In other programming languages like C, a boolean data type is declared as an int and can be incremented or decremented. In Java, to toggle a boolean value, we can use the boolean toggle operator (!), which turns a true value into a false one and vice versa. This is the correct version:

```
boolean doorIsOpen = false;
// I want to open the door,
doorIsOpen = !doorIsOpen;  // this one is correct
```

   For boolean values, false is the default value.

3.7 The Math Class

The java.lang.Math class is essential in Java programming as it provides a collection of methods for performing mathematical operations that are commonly needed in development. Its significance lies in the ability to handle tasks like calculations, trigonometry, exponential functions, logarithms, and more without having to implement complex algorithms manually.

Knowing about the `Math` class helps programmers efficiently solve problems, write cleaner code, and handle calculations that are integral to many programming tasks.

The `Math` class can be found under the `java.lang` package, and since it's inside the `java.lang` package is automatically accessible to us. The `Math` class contains the commonly used methods for mathematical computation, and all of these methods are static.

That's why whenever we access any of these methods, we need to access them by the name of the class. So if you want to use the absolute value method abs(), you need to prefix it with `Math` followed by a dot, and then the name of the method, and then you could start passing the parameter.

Below are some of the commonly used `Math` methods:

`abs()`	- computes for the absolute value
`cbrt()`	- computes for the cube root value
`sqrt()`	- computes for the square root value
`ceil()`	- Rounds a decimal number up to the nearest integer
`floor()`	- Rounds a decimal number down to the nearest integer
`min()`	- returns the smaller value between the two parameters
`max()`	- returns the larger value between the two parameters

pow()   - computes the exponential value of the first
              parameter raised to the value of the second
              parameter.

random() - returns a random value from 0.0 up to less
              than 1.0

round()   - performs rounding off values.

To test these methods, try coding them by using either a
text editor, an IDE, or even an online compiler.

Figure 3.4 **Set of selected Math Methods with output**

```
 6    System.out.println(Math.abs(3));          // 3
 7    System.out.println(Math.abs(-3));         // 3
 8
 9    System.out.println(Math.cbrt(27));        // 3.0
10    System.out.println(Math.sqrt(36));        // 6.0
11
12    System.out.println(Math.ceil(3.1));       // 4.0
13    System.out.println(Math.floor(3.1));      // 3.0
14
15    System.out.println(Math.max(100, 200));   // 200
16    System.out.println(Math.min(100, 200));   // 100
17
18    System.out.println(Math.pow(2, 3));       // 8.0
19    System.out.println(Math.round(3.1));      // 3
20    System.out.println(Math.random());        // any value from 0.0 up to < 1.0
```

To get the complete list of Math methods, check out the
Java API Documentation.

3.8 The Scanner Class

Let's discuss how to use the Scanner class from the
java.util package for handling user input in Java. This
class simplifies the process of gathering various types of
input from the keyboard, such as int, double, and String.
It provides an easy method to read values and allows
developers to interact with users in a Java program.

Table 3.6 shows the different input methods under the Scanner class.

Table 3.6 **Scanner next() methods**

Data Types	nextXxx methods
byte	nextByte()
short	nextShort()
int	nextInt()
long	nextLong()
float	nextFloat()
double	nextDouble()
char	next().charAt(0)
boolean	nextBoolean()
Single String	next()
Strings with spaces	nextLine()

The Scanner class can be accessed by importing the java.util.Scanner at the beginning of your code. Once imported, you can create a Scanner object to read input. For example, sc.next() is used for retrieving a single word input, while sc.nextLine() handles a full line of text, useful for reading names with spaces. For numeric input, like age, the sc.nextInt() method is ideal, and you can easily display the results using System.out.println(). After input processing is complete, it's important to close the Scanner object with sc.close() to prevent resource leaks. The following is an example of a simple Java program that reads a user's name and age and prints a message with the incremented age for the next year.

```
1  // Filename: KeyboardInput.java
2  import java.util.Scanner;
3
4  public class KeyboardInput {
5
6     public static void main(String[] args) {
7
8           Scanner sc = new Scanner(System.in);
9           System.out.println("What is your name?");
10          String name = sc.next();
11
12          System.out.println("How old are you?");
13          int age = sc.nextInt();
14
15          System.out.println("Hello " + name +
16                             ", next year you'll be " +
17                             (age + 1) + " years old.");
18
19          sc.close();
20     }
21 }
```

Chapter Summary

- There are three (3) types of Java comments:
  - The single-line comment (//)
  - The multi-line comment (/* */)
  - The Javadoc (Java Documentation) comment (/** */)

- Semicolons are used to end an expression or a Java statement.

- Blocks are pairs of curly braces ({ }) that are used to denote the body of a class, method, or a body of a control structure.

- White spaces refer to spaces, tabs, and enter keys. They are irrelevant in your Java source code but are used to improve the readability of your code.

- Java identifiers are used to identify classes, methods, and variables.

- There are 57 Java keywords at present.

- There are two special keywords that are not used. `const` and `goto` cannot be used even in future versions of Java.

- There are eight primitive data types in the Java Programming Language: `byte`, `short`, `int`, `long`, `float`, `double`, `char`, and `boolean`.

- The `Math` class contains the commonly used mathematical methods used for math computations like the methods used for trigonometric functions, rounding off, and computing exponential values.

- The `Scanner` class is one of the several ways to accept user input in Java. It is also the easiest and preferred way, as it allows the user to accept a pre-formatted input.

Quiz

1. Which of these is NOT a Primitive Data Type?
   a. String
   b. double
   c. int
   d. char

2. What symbol do you put at the end of a number if you want to assign it to a variable of type long?
   a. F
   b. L
   c. D
   d. X

3. What makes a double different from an int?
   a. A double can't have decimal values
   b. There is no difference between a double and an int
   c. A double can't be negative
   d. A double can have decimal values

4. What are the differences between the four integral data types (byte, short, int, and long)?
   a. They occupy different amounts of memory space (bits). Which means they have different ranges of values that they can represent.
   b. Some cannot be changed
   c. Only some can represent decimals
   d. Some cannot represent negative numbers

5. Which import statement MUST be present if you are going to use the Scanner class in your code?

   a. import java.lang.Scanner;
   b. import java.awt.Scanner;
   c. import java.io.Scanner;
   d. import java.util.Scanner;

6. Which of the following IS NOT a Java Comment?

   a. /** This is a comment */
   b. /* This is a comment */
   c. // This is a comment
   d. # This is a comment

7. Which of the following IS NOT a Java keyword?

   a. goto
   b. null
   c. const
   d. public

8. You are creating a class that will represent a mobile phone. Knowing the Java coding convention, how would you declare a public class that will represent an object for mobile phones?

   a. public class mobile phone {}
   b. public class mobilePhone {}
   c. public class MobilePhone {}
   d. public class MOBILEPHONE {}

9. What is the output of the statement `System.out.`
   `println(Math.floor(-3.1));`?
   a. -3
   b. -4
   c. -4.0
   d. -3.0

10. For every mobile phone, there is a mobile phone
    number. You were tasked to write a code that will
    contain a variable that will represent the mobile
    phone number of type long. How will you declare the
    variable by using the right coding convention?
    a. long MobilePhoneNumber;
    b. long mobile_phone_number;
    c. long mobilePhoneNumber;
    d. long mobilePhoneNumberL;

Answers

1 - a	2 - b	3 - d	4 - a	5 - d
6 - d	7 - b	8 - c	9 - c	10 - c

Coding Tasks

Coding Task 1:

Declare the following variables with the corresponding data types and initial values based on the given table below.

Variable Name	Data Type	Initial Value
discounted price	float	75.89
final grade	double	1.25
gender	char	f
full name	string	Michelle Decamora
number of levels	byte	20
is logged in	boolean	true
birth year	int	1988

Create a Java program and display all the declared variables and their corresponding values. Use the correct naming convention in naming these variables.

Coding Task 2:

Create a Java Program that will ask the user to enter two int values. Display the larger value between the two input values. Use the method `max()` found in the `Math` class.

Coding Task 3:

Welcome Banner with Comments and Proper Formatting

Problem:

Write a Java program that prints a simple welcome banner to the console using proper use of comments, semicolons, white spaces, and block formatting. The program should demonstrate all three types of Java comments: single-line, multi-line, and Javadoc comments.

Requirements:

- Use all three types of comments in the code
- Properly format the code with semicolons, blocks {}, and consistent indentation
- Use meaningful identifiers following Java naming conventions

Expected Output:

```
====================
Welcome to Java!
Let's start coding!
====================
```

Coding Task 4:

Basic Math Computation with Primitive Data Types

Problem:

Write a program that declares variables using primitive data types to store the radius of a circle, computes the area and circumference, and displays the result. Use the Math class to access Math.PI. Your program should also ask the user to input the value for the radius, which is a whole number, and use the correct data type for all variables.

Requirements:

- Use appropriate primitive data types (double, int)
- Use constants where appropriate, use the Java API Documentation, and use the Math class to use the constant PI.

Expected Output:

```
Input the value for the radius: 5 <ENTER>
Area: 78.54
Circumference: 31.42

(Assuming radius = 5, Area = п * r², Circumference = 2 * п * r)
```

Coding Task 5:

User Input with Scanner and Type Conversion

Problem:

Create a program that asks the user to enter their name and age. Then, display a personalized greeting along with their age in months. This task demonstrates the use of the Scanner class and basic arithmetic.

Requirements:

- Import and use the Scanner class for user input
- Read a String and an int value from the user
- Compute the age in months (age * 12)
- Follow Java identifier naming conventions

Expected Output (Sample Run):

```
Enter your name: Danielle <ENTER>
Enter your age: 20 <ENTER>
Hello, Danielle! You are approximately 240 months old.
```

Practice More, Get Better!

Additional coding tasks for this chapter are available in the exclusive online resources that accompany this book.

CHAPTER 4
Java Operators

Key Learning Objectives

- Recognize and correctly use all major categories of Java operators: arithmetic, relational, logical, assignment, unary, ternary, and bitwise.
- Understand the function and behavior of each operator in practical code examples.
- Apply compound assignment operators to simplify expressions.
- Use the ternary operator as a concise alternative to simple conditional statements.
- Comprehend the concept of operator precedence and associativity in Java expressions.
- Predict the outcome of complex expressions by correctly applying the rules of operator precedence.
- Debug common logic errors related to operator misuse or misunderstanding of precedence.
- Use parentheses effectively to control or clarify the order of operations in expressions.

In this chapter, you will explore the full range of operators available in Java, from basic arithmetic and assignment to more advanced constructs like logical operators and bitwise manipulation. You'll learn not only how each operator works individually but also how multiple operators interact within a single expression. A central focus will be understanding Java's operator precedence — the rules that determine the order in which operations are evaluated. Misunderstanding precedence is a common source of bugs, so this chapter will help you develop a strong grasp of how Java interprets expressions. By the end of this chapter, you'll be able to write cleaner, more accurate code and understand the subtle behaviors of complex expressions with confidence.

4.1 Java Operators

Table 4.1 shows the complete list of Java operators. The top row has a higher order of precedence than the rows at the bottom.

Table 4.1 **List of Java operators**

Operators	Associativity
(`<data_type>`) [ ] . ! ~ unary- unary+ - - ++	L to R
* / %	L to R
+ -	L to R
<< >> >>>	L to R
< > <= >= instanceof	L to R
= = ! =	L to R
&	L to R
^	L to R
|	L to R
&&	L to R
| |	L to R
`<boolean_exp>` ? `<value_if_true>` : `<value_if_false>`	R to L
= *= /= %= += -= <<= >>= >>>= &= ^= |=	R to L

Let us discuss how each operator works.

1. Casting (`<data_type>`)

Data type casting in Java refers to converting one data type into another. This is done to make data compatible with specific operations or to match the expected data type in a given context. Casting can be applied to either primitive data types or reference types. In this section, we will first talk about casting for primitive types. The casting for reference data types will be discussed in Volume 2 of this series.

Data type casting is the process of converting a value from one data type to another, i.e., either widening or narrowing its declared data type. There are two ways to do a cast. It can be done implicitly or explicitly. Implicit casting means you are letting Java do the automatic cast for you. While in explicit casting, you are the one writing or dictating how the cast should be done.

Implicit cast follows a certain rule. It follows the hierarchy shown in Figure 4.1.

Figure 4.1 Primitive data type hierarchy

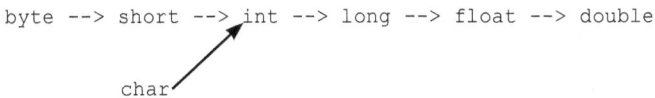

```
byte --> short --> int --> long --> float --> double

        char
```

This means that, once a primitive variable undergoes an implicit cast, it gets promoted (or demoted) following the data type hierarchy. For example, a `byte` can be cast to become an `int`.

Here's an example:

```
1    public class Casting1 {
2
3        public static void main(String[] args) {
4
5            byte b1 = 10;
6            byte b2 = 5;
7            byte b3 = b1 + b2;
8
9            System.out.println("B3 = " + b3);
10       }
11   }
```

If you look closely, you would potentially see the following error:

```
Casting1.java:7: possible loss of precision
found    : int
required: byte
            byte b3 = b1 + b2;
                      ^
1 error
```

Notice the type of error? It says, **possible loss of precision**, which means it is an error that has something to do with primitive casts. If ignored, it can lose its precision. The error occurs because in Java, arithmetic operations like addition (b1 + b2) are automatically promoted or upcast to an int even if the operands are declared as byte. In line 5 and in line 6, both b1 and b2 were declared as byte. However, when it reached line 7, it caused an error because b1 and b2 were implicitly (automatically) cast before the addition took place in line 7. At this point, you are actually adding an int and an int and attempting to store them inside a byte. Java promotes byte to int implicitly in any mathematical operation, in this case, the addition operation; thus, the error **possible loss of precision** occurred.

So, instead of doing it the following way:

```
7        byte b3 = b1 + b2;
```

It should be done this way:

```
7        byte b3 = (byte)(b1 + b2);
```

Try recompiling this code and running it, you should have no problems anymore.

Explicit casting was applied in **byte b3 = (byte) (b1 + b2)**. Explicit casting requires manual intervention because it involves converting a larger data type into a smaller one. Since there is a possibility of losing information or precision, you must explicitly specify the type to which you want to convert.

What happened here is that b1 and b2 were declared as byte, and before you can join two variables together via a mathematical operator, they need to be in their default data type. This means that before b1 is added to b2, b1, which is a byte, will then be upcasted automatically to an int. After which, b2 will follow the same pattern. Only when both b1 and b2 are of type int can you add up their values.

In conclusion, data type casting in Java is a fundamental concept that ensures compatibility between data types during operations, especially between smaller and larger primitive types. Understanding when and how to use implicit and explicit casting is essential to avoid common errors like "possible loss of precision," which often arise during arithmetic operations involving byte, short, or char types.

2. The [ ] Index Operator

In Java, the index operator [] is used to access specific elements in an array by their position.

For instance, if you have an array like:

```
int[] numbers = {10, 20, 30};
```

You can retrieve the second element using `numbers[1]`, which returns 20. This same concept applies to the `main` method's parameter in Java: `String[] args`. This parameter allows the program to receive an array of strings as input from the command line. Each individual argument passed can then be accessed using the index operator—for example, `args[0]` refers to the first argument, `args[1]` to the second, and so on. Chapter 7 will provide a more comprehensive discussion on Arrays.

3. The dot (.) Operator

The dot (.) operator is used to call an instance member of an object. Let's say we have a given class Person;

```
1   public class Person {
2
3       public String name = "noname";
4       public int age = 0;
5       . . . .
32      public Person addAge(int moreAge) {
33
             . . . .
37      }
38      public String toString() {
39
             . . . .
41      }
42  }
```

In line 6 of our test class (as shown in the example below), we use the dot operator to call an instance method `toString()`, using the object `p1`.

```
1   public class TestPerson {
2
3       public static void main(String[] args) {
4
5           Person p1 = new Person();
6           System.out.println(p1.toString());
```

```
7      }
8  }
```

4. The `boolean` Toggle (`!`) Operator

This operator is used to negate (or toggle) a `boolean` value. Here's a sample code snippet.

```
boolean isOpen = true;
System.out.println(!isOpen);
```

Output:

```
false
```

5. The Binary Toggle (`~`) Operator

In many computing scenarios, it's important to understand how decimal values are represented in binary form. This is especially useful when dealing with low-level operations such as bitwise manipulation, setting or clearing flags, or understanding how data is stored in memory. For example, suppose we want to toggle specific bits in a number or simply observe its binary representation. To do that, we first need to convert the decimal number to binary.

First, change the decimal value to its binary equivalent.

In decimal (base 10) format, you have:

```
1357
```

In binary (base 2) format, you have:

| 0 | 0 | 0 | 0 | 0 | 0 | 0 | 0 | 0 | 0 | 0 | 0 | 0 | 0 | 0 | 0 | 0 | 0 | 0 | 1 | 0 | 1 | 0 | 1 | 0 | 0 | 1 | 1 | 0 | 1 |

`~1357` will toggle all the binary bits, all 1's will be 0's, and all 0's will be 1's

| 1 | 1 | 1 | 1 | 1 | 1 | 1 | 1 | 1 | 1 | 1 | 1 | 1 | 1 | 1 | 1 | 1 | 1 | 1 | 0 | 1 | 0 | 1 | 0 | 1 | 1 | 0 | 0 | 1 | 0 |

After toggling all binary bits, convert them back to their decimal format.

```
~1357 = -1358
```

6. Pre or Post-Increment (++) Operator

This operator increments the value of the variable by 1, the only difference is the timing. Pre increment (++a) will increment the value first, then you can use the incremented value afterwards, while post increment (a++) will allow you to use the original value first, after using the original value, you increment it by 1.

```
int a = 0, b = 0;
System.out.println("a = " + ++a);
System.out.println("b = " + b++);

System.out.println("a = " + a);
System.out.println("b = " + b);
```

Output:

```
a = 1
b = 0
a = 1
b = 1
```

7. Pre or Post-Decrement (--) Operator

This operator decrements the value of the variable by 1. Just like the (++) operator, the difference is the timing. Pre-decrement (--a) will decrement the value first, then you can use the decremented value afterwards, while post-decrement (a--) will allow you to use the original value first, after using the original value, you decrement it by 1. For example:

```
int a = 0, b = 0;
System.out.println("a = " + --a);
System.out.println("b = " + b--);

System.out.println("a = " + a);
System.out.println("b = " + b);
```

Will give you an output of:

```
a = -1
```

```
b = 0
a = -1
b = -1
```

8. The `unary +` and `unary -` Operators

These are used for stating a positive value or a negative value.

For example:

```
int x = +5;
int y = -5;
```

9. The Multiplication (*) Operator

Used to get the product of two expressions. For example:

```
int num1 = 10;
int num2 = 3;

int num3 = num1 * num2;

System.out.println("Num3: " + num3);
```

Will give you an output of:

```
Num3: 30
```

10. The Division (/) Operator

Used to get the quotient of two numbers. For example:

```
int num1 = 10;
int num2 = 3;

int num3 = num1 / num2;

System.out.println("Num3: " + num3);
```

Will give you an output of:

```
Num3: 3
```

Why did we have **Num3: 3** as the output here? The output that we are expecting should be Num3: 3.333, right?

Let's check the given values of num1 and num2, which are 10 and 3, respectively. Since the numerator and the denominator are both integer values, the result will also be an integer value. So if you want to get the exact double output, one of your operands must be a double. Consider this example:

```
int num1 = 10;
int num2 = 3;
double num3 = (double)num1 / num2;
System.out.println("Num3: " + num3);
```

Therefore, the output here will be:

```
Num3: 3.3333333333333335
```

Now, that's the exact double value.

In the line: double num3 = **(double)num1** / num2; num1 was explicitly cast to a double, allowing the operation **(double)num1** / num2 to result in a double value.

11. The Modulo (%) Operator

It is used to get the remainder of two numbers. It can be applied to any numeric primitive data type. For example:

```
int num1 = 10;
int num2 = 3;
int num3 = num1 % num2;
System.out.println("Num3: " + num3);
```

This will give you an output of:

```
Num3: 1
```

What if both the operands are double values? Can we still use the modulo operator? In Java, YES, we can, unlike in other programming languages, say in C and C++, where using double values for the modulo operation is not allowed. For example:

```
double num1 = 2.25;
double num2 = 0.5;

double num3 = num1 % num2;

System.out.println("Num3: " + num3);
```

This will give you this output:

```
Num3: 0.25
```

12. The Addition or Concatenation (+) Operator

The (+) operator is used to get the sum of two operands. It can also be used to concatenate String values. Thus, it is an example of an overloaded operator (an overloaded operator is an operator that may have two or more functions depending on the given operands).

An example of the use of the addition operator:

```
int num1 = 10;
int num2 = 3;

int num3 = num1 + num2;

System.out.println("Num3: " + num3);
```

The output is:

```
Num3: 13
```

An example of the use of the concatenation operator:

```
5    System.out.println(10 + 5);
6    System.out.println("10" + "5");
```

```
7      System.out.println("abc" + "def");
8      System.out.println("abc" + 10 + 5);
9      System.out.println(10 + 5 + "abc");
10     System.out.println("abc" + (10 + 5));
```

Examine each line of code and predict the output. Now check your answers:

```
15
105
abcdef
abc105
15abc
abc15
```

In the code snippet provided, implicit casting to String occurs when non-String types are concatenated with a String.

- Line 8: "abc" + 10 + 5 starts with a String, so both 10 and 5 are implicitly cast to String during concatenation, resulting in "abc105".

- Line 9: 10 + 5 + "abc" starts with integers, so 10 + 5 is calculated as 15, which is then implicitly cast to String and concatenated with "abc", resulting in "15abc".

- Line 10: ("abc" + (10 + 5)) evaluates the expression 10 + 5 first, resulting in 15, and then casts 15 to String during concatenation with "abc", producing "abc15".

13. The Subtraction (–) Operator

The subtraction operator is used to get the difference between two operands.

```
int num1 = 10;
int num2 = 3;

int num3 = num1 - num2;

System.out.println("Num3: " + num3);
```

This will give you an output of:

```
Num3: 7
```

14. The Shift Left (<<) Operator

The shift left operator will shift all significant bits to the left based on the value indicated.

Consider the given values:

```
int x = 13;
System.out.println(x << 2);
```

The binary value of x will be shifted 2 binary spaces to the left, giving us an output of 52.

The solution:

	64	32	16	8	4	2	1
13 << 2				1	1	0	1
52		1	1	0	1	0	0

15. The Shift Right (>>) Operator

This will shift all significant bits to the right.

```
int x = 13;
System.out.println(x >> 2);
```

This will give you an output of 3.
The solution:

	16	8	4	2	1		
13 >> 2		1	1	0	1		
3				1	1	0	1

You have to shift all significant bits two spaces to the right; whatever bits that go out of bounds are dropped.

16. The Unsigned Shift Right (>>>) Operators

Unlike the previous two operators (shift left and shift right), the unsigned shift right operator is unique only to Java. This is how it works.

```
int x = 1357;
System.out.println(x >>> 5);
```

Since x is declared as an `int`, we will use 32 bits. Then, we will use an unsigned shift right to shift all significant bits to the right 5 spaces.

The solution:

```
1357
```

`0 0 0 0 0 0 0 0 0 0 0 0 0 0 0 0 0 0 0 0 0 1 0 1 0 1 0 0 1 1 0 1`

```
1357 >>> 5
```

`0 0 0 0 0 0 0 0 0 0 0 0 0 0 0 0 0 0 0 0 0 0 0 0 0 0 1 0 1 0 1 0`

```
Answer is: 42
```

So, what's the difference between the shift right (>>) and the unsigned shift right (>>>) operators? The difference is the treatment of negative numbers. Compare the following:

```
1357
```

`0 0 0 0 0 0 0 0 0 0 0 0 0 0 0 0 0 0 0 0 0 1 0 1 0 1 0 0 1 1 0 1`

In Java, negative binary numbers are represented using the *two's complement*. This method reserves the leftmost bit as the sign bit, where 0 indicates positive and 1 indicates negative. To compute the *two's complement* of a number, you invert all the bits (change 0s to 1s and vice versa) and then add 1 to the inverted value. This approach allows for simple binary arithmetic operations and eliminates the need for a separate subtraction operation. It also makes it easier for Java to handle negative values with the same set of instructions as positive values. For example:

```
-1357
```

| 1 | 1 | 1 | 1 | 1 | 1 | 1 | 1 | 1 | 1 | 1 | 1 | 1 | 1 | 1 | 1 | 1 | 1 | 1 | 1 | 1 | 0 | 1 | 0 | 1 | 0 | 1 | 1 | 0 | 0 | 1 | 1 |

1357 >> 5 is the same as

| 0 | 0 | 0 | 0 | 0 | 0 | 0 | 0 | 0 | 0 | 0 | 0 | 0 | 0 | 0 | 0 | 0 | 0 | 0 | 0 | 0 | 0 | 0 | 0 | 0 | 0 | 1 | 0 | 1 | 0 | 1 | 0 |

1357 >>> 5 because you are using the >> and the >>> operators on positive numbers.

| 0 | 0 | 0 | 0 | 0 | 0 | 0 | 0 | 0 | 0 | 0 | 0 | 0 | 0 | 0 | 0 | 0 | 0 | 0 | 0 | 0 | 0 | 0 | 0 | 0 | 0 | 1 | 0 | 1 | 0 | 1 | 0 |

Negative values such as -1357 >> 5 will have a different output than

| 1 | 1 | 1 | 1 | 1 | 1 | 1 | 1 | 1 | 1 | 1 | 1 | 1 | 1 | 1 | 1 | 1 | 1 | 1 | 1 | 1 | 1 | 1 | 1 | 1 | 0 | 1 | 0 | 1 | 0 | 1 |

-1357 >>> 5 because you are using the unsigned shift right >>> operator.

| 0 | 0 | 0 | 0 | 0 | 1 | 1 | 1 | 1 | 1 | 1 | 1 | 1 | 1 | 1 | 1 | 1 | 1 | 1 | 1 | 1 | 1 | 1 | 1 | 1 | 1 | 0 | 1 | 0 | 1 | 0 | 1 |

Notice that even the *sign bit* moved, thus the name, unsigned shift right.

The *sign bit* is the leftmost bit in the binary representation of a number and is used to indicate whether the number is positive or negative. This concept is essential in computer systems when representing signed numbers, where both positive and negative values need to be encoded in binary. For positive values, the *sign bit* is 0, while for negative values, the *sign bit* is 1.

Bitwise operations operate at the level of their individual bits. On older microprocessors, bitwise operations are slightly faster than addition and subtraction and usually faster than multiplication and division.

In modern architecture, this is not always the case; bitwise operations are generally of the same speed as addition but still faster than multiplication.

Also, it is worth mentioning that even if we have the unsigned shift right (>>>) operator, we do not have an unsigned shift left operator (<<<).

17. The Relational (Comparison) Operators

Learning to use relational operators in Java is essential because they form the foundation of decision-making in programming. These operators compare two values and determine the relationship between them, such as whether one value is greater than, less than, equal to, or not equal to another. The results of these comparisons are boolean values (true or false), which are used to control the flow of a program.

For example:

- Relational operators help us write conditional statements (if, else if, while, etc.), which allow programs to respond dynamically based on input or conditions.

- They are crucial in implementing loops, where the continuation of the loop depends on a specific condition being met.

A simple example is checking if a user's age is above 18 to determine if they are eligible to vote:

```
if (age >= 18) {
    System.out.println("You are eligible to vote.");
} else {
    System.out.println("You are not eligible to vote.");
}
```

Without relational operators, it would be impossible to write programs that adapt to varying conditions, making them a fundamental part of Java programming.

The less than (<), greater than (>), less than or equal to (<=), greater than or equal to (>=), and instanceof operators are all used to test the values of the operands against each other. All the above-mentioned operators will give you a boolean value in return. The instanceof operator will be discussed in a more detailed manner in the second volume of this book.

18. The Exactly Equal To (==) and the Not Equal To (!=) Operators

In Java, when you need to compare two values, you can use relational operators. Two common ones are the "exactly equal to" (==) operator and the "not equal to" (!=) operator.

The == operator checks whether two values are the same. If they are equal, it returns `true`; otherwise, it returns `false`.

On the other hand, the != operator checks whether two values are different. It returns `true` if the values are not equal, and `false` if they are the same.

These operators are often used in decision-making structures like if statements to control the flow of a program based on comparisons.

19. The Bitwise AND (&) Operator

Learning about bitwise operators in Java is important because they allow us to manipulate data at the bit level, which is essential in scenarios that require high performance, low-level operations, or precise control over data.

This example demonstrates how the bitwise AND (&) operator can be used in Java to determine whether a number is even or odd by checking the least significant bit (LSB) of its binary representation:

- If the LSB is 0, the number is even.
- If the LSB is 1, the number is odd.

We can use the bitwise AND (&) operator to check this by performing num & 1. If the result is 0, the number is even; otherwise, it's odd.

```
int num = 7;
if ((number & 1) == 0) {
    System.out.println(num + " is even.");
```

```
    } else {
        System.out.println(num + " is odd.");
    }
```

Explanation:

- The binary representation of 7 is 0111.

- Performing 7 & 1 results in 0001 because only the LSB is compared.

- Since the result is not 0, the program concludes that 7 is odd.

This is a quick and efficient way to check for even or odd numbers without using modulus (%).

Consider another example of how bitwise AND (&) works.

```
int x = 13, y = 9;
System.out.println(x & y);
```

Output:

```
9
```

To perform a bitwise AND (&) operation, we first convert each operand to its binary representation and then compare each pair of corresponding bits from the two binary numbers. The rule is simple: the result bit is 1 only if **both** bits being compared are 1; otherwise, the result bit is 0.

Let's break it down using this example:

```
x = 1101 (which is 13 in decimal)
y = 1001 (which is 9 in decimal)
```

Now, apply the bitwise AND operation:

```
  1101
& 1001
  ------
  1001
```

Here's how it works, bit by bit:

- `1 & 1 = 1`
- `1 & 0 = 0`
- `0 & 0 = 0`
- `1 & 1 = 1`

So, the result is `1001`, which is `9` in decimal.

The bitwise AND operation compares each bit of the operands and keeps a `1` only in the positions where both original bits were `1`. In this case, the result of `1101 & 1001` is `1001`, or `9` in decimal.

20. The Bitwise OR (|) Operator

Just like the bitwise AND `(&)` operator, the bitwise OR operator `(|)` in Java is also useful because it allows us to perform operations that manipulate data directly at the bit level, enabling more control over how data is processed or stored.

The bitwise OR `(|)` operator can also be used to combine multiple conditions in situations like managing permissions or flags. By combining multiple bits, you can efficiently represent and check for multiple conditions at once.

In the UNIX filesystem, there are file permissions, and we can use the bitwise OR `(|)` operator to combine permissions.

```
int readPermission = 1;      // Binary: 0001
int writePermission = 2;     // Binary: 0010
int executePermission = 4;   // Binary: 0100

// Combine read and write permissions
int userPermissions = readPermission | writePermission;
```

Here, `userPermissions` will enable both read and write permissions.

Consider another example of how bitwise OR `(|)` works.

```
int x = 13, y = 9;
System.out.println(x | y);
```

To perform a bitwise OR (|) operation, we first convert each operand into its binary form, then compare each pair of corresponding bits. The rule for OR is straightforward: the result bit is 1 if at least one of the bits being compared is 1; otherwise, the result is 0.

Let's break it down using this example:

```
x = 1101 (which is 13 in decimal)
y = 1001 (which is 9 in decimal)
```

Now, apply the bitwise OR operation:

```
    1101
|   1001
    ------
    1101
```

Let's go through this bit by bit:
- 1 | 1 = 1
- 1 | 0 = 1
- 0 | 0 = 0
- 1 | 1 = 1

So, the result is 1101 in binary, which is 13 in decimal.

The bitwise OR operation compares each bit of the two operands and produces 1 in every position where at least one of the bits is 1. In this case, 1101 | 1001 gives 1101, or 13 in decimal, showing that the OR operation keeps all the 1's from both operands.

21. The Bitwise XOR (^) Operator

Just like the bitwise AND (&) operator and the bitwise OR operator (|), the bitwise XOR operator (^) in Java is important because it provides a powerful tool for performing operations that involve toggling or flipping specific bits in a binary number. XOR is useful in scenarios where you need to compare or change bits in a way that isn't possible with standard arithmetic or logical operators.

A clever use of XOR is swapping two values without needing a temporary variable. By XORing two numbers twice, you can exchange their values.

Example: Swapping values without using a temporary variable.

```java
int x = 5, y = 10;
System.out.println("x: " + x + ", y: " + y);
// Output: x: 5, y: 10

x = x ^ y; // Step 1
y = x ^ y; // Step 2
x = x ^ y; // Step 3

System.out.println("x: " + x + ", y: " + y);
// Output: x: 10, y: 5
```

Consider another example of how bitwise XOR (^) works.

```java
int x = 13, y = 9;
System.out.println(x ^ y);
```

To perform a bitwise XOR (^) operation, we begin by converting each operand to its binary form, then comparing each pair of corresponding bits. For XOR, the result is 1 only if the bits are different; if they're the same (both 0 or both 1), the result is 0.

Let's break it down using this example:

```
x = 1101 (which is 13 in decimal)
y = 1001 (which is 9 in decimal)
```

Now, perform the XOR operation:

```
    1101
^   1001
    ------
    0100
```

Let's break this down bit by bit:

- `1 ^ 1 = 0` → (same bits)
- `1 ^ 0 = 1` → (different bits)
- `0 ^ 0 = 0` → (same bits)
- `1 ^ 1 = 0` → (same bits)

So, the result is `0100` in binary, which is 4 in decimal.

The XOR operator highlights the differences between two values at the bit level. In this case, `1101 ^ 1001` results in `0100`, or 4 in decimal—showing that only the second bit (from the right) differs between the two inputs.

Bitwise operators in Java play a vital role in low-level programming, enabling precise manipulation of data at the bit level. They are essential for tasks like optimizing memory usage, implementing efficient algorithms, and performing operations on binary data. Their applications are widespread in fields such as cryptography, graphics processing, and communication protocols, where performance and efficiency are critical. By using these operators, developers can create more efficient and compact code, leading to faster execution and reduced resource consumption in various applications.

22. The Logical AND Operator (&) vs. the Short-Circuit AND Operator (&&)

A key difference is that `&&` employs short-circuit evaluation, meaning if the first condition is false, the second condition isn't evaluated, whereas `&` evaluates both operands regardless.

The logical and operator (&)

```
int a = 5, b = 10;
System.out.println((a < 5) & (++b != 10));
System.out.println("a = " + a + "\tb = " + b);
```

Will give you an output of:

```
false
a = 5      b = 11
```

This operator always evaluates both conditions, even if the first one is already `false`. That's why in the first example, ++b is still executed, increasing the value of b.

The short circuit and operator (&&)

```
int a = 5, b = 10;
System.out.println((a < 5) && (++b != 10));
System.out.println("a = " + a + "\tb = " + b);
```

Will give you an output of:

```
false
a = 5      b = 10
```

This operator is smarter—it only evaluates the second condition if the first one is `true`. If the first condition is `false`, it skips the second one completely. That's why in the second example, ++b is not executed, and b remains unchanged.

In summary, use & when you always want both sides to be evaluated. Use && when you want to skip unnecessary evaluation for performance or to avoid side effects.

23. The Logical OR Operator (|) vs. the Short-Circuit OR Operator (| |)

On the other hand, the | | operator is a short-circuit OR operator that evaluates two boolean expressions. It returns `true` if at least one of the conditions is `true` and utilizes short-circuit evaluation, meaning if the first expression is true, the second is not evaluated anymore, while the logical or operator | evaluates both expressions regardless of the results.

The logical or operator (|)

```
int a = 5, b = 10;
System.out.println((a <= 5) | (++b != 10));
System.out.println("a = " + a + "\tb = " + b);
```

Will give you an output of:

```
true
a = 5     b = 11
```

This operator always evaluates both sides of the expression, even if the first condition is already true.

In our example, since a <= 5 is true, Java still executes ++b, increasing b from 10 to 11.

The short circuit or operator (||)

```
int a = 5, b = 10;
System.out.println((a <= 5) || (++b != 10));
System.out.println("a = " + a + "\tb = " + b);
```

Will give you an output of:

```
true
a = 5     b = 10
```

This operator only evaluates the second condition if the first one is false. Since a <= 5 is already true, Java skips the second condition, so ++b is not executed, and b remains 10.

In summary, use | when you always want both sides to run, regardless of the first result. Use || when you want to skip the second part if the first condition is already enough to determine the result.

24. The Ternary Operator (e1 ? e2 : e3)

The ternary operator can be used as a substitute for a simple if-else statement, which will be discussed in the next chapter, including all its variations.

Consider the following sample code snippet:

```
int quiz = 70;
if (quiz >= 70)
        System.out.println("Pass");
else
        System.out.println("Fail");
```

Let's use the ternary operator to rewrite the code snippet.

```
System.out.println((quiz >= 70) ? "Pass" : "Fail");
```

25. Shorthand Operators

Shorthand operators are used as a substitute for Java assignment operators.

Table 4.2 | List of Longhand and Shorthand Operators

Longhand Operators	Equivalent Shorthand Operators
a = a * 2	a *= 2
a = a / 2	a /= 2
a = a % 2	a %= 2
a = a + 2	a += 2
a = a - 2	a -= 2
a = a << 2	a <<= 2
a = a >> 2	a >>= 2
a = a >>> 2	a >>>= 2
a = a & 2	a &= 2
a = a ^ 2	a ^= 2
a = a | 2	a |= 2

4.2 Order of Precedence

The list of operators that you have just seen follows a certain set of rules in execution. Those rules are what we call the 'order of precedence'. These rules will ensure that once you have this set of operators inside a certain expression or statement, it will execute a set of operators first, followed by another, and then by another.

The order in which the operators are stated in *Figure 4.1: List of Java Operators* also shows the order of precedence. The operators listed on top have a higher priority compared to the ones on the lower row.

Here is an example involving several operators: the (++) increment, the (/) division, the (+) addition, and the (=) assignment operators.

Say you have the following snippet:

```
int a = 5, b = 10, c = 4;        // 1
int x = a + b / ++c;             // 2
System.out.println(x);           // 3
```

Once executed in a valid Java file, you should get an output of: 7.

In the above code snippet, the expression on line 2 calculates the value of x. The order of operations (or precedence) dictates that division occurs before addition.

The pre-increment operator ++c increases c from 4 to 5. Next, b / c is evaluated, which is 10 / 5, yielding 2.

Finally, the addition is performed: a + 2, or 5 + 2, resulting in 7.

Thus, the output is 7.

The order of precedence can be changed by the use of the grouping symbol, a parentheses (). Whatever mathematical expression is placed inside the parentheses will be the top priority. Consider the same snippet, this time a parenthesis is placed in line 2.

```
int a = 5, b = 10, c = 4;        // 1
int x = (a + b) / ++c;           // 2
System.out.println(x);           // 3
```

In this version, the order of operations in line 2 will change. We now evaluate `(a + b)` first, followed by the incrementation of the value of c (++c), then the division (`/`) of the sum of a and b with the new value of c (`10 / 5`), and lastly the assignment operator (=). This will then print a value of 3 as the output in line 3.

In an event that the parentheses contain another parenthesis inside, the evaluation should be done from the innermost parentheses, followed by the outer parentheses. Consider this example:

```
int x = ((a + b) - c) / d;
```

The first that will be evaluated will be `(a + b)`, followed by subtracting the value of c, then whatever value you get will be the numerator, and the value of d will be the denominator. Lastly, the result will be assigned to x.

This chapter introduced you to the full range of Java operators, from fundamental arithmetic operations to more advanced bitwise and ternary logic. You learned how each operator functions and how they are used in practical code, especially when combined within complex expressions. A key focus was understanding operator precedence and associativity, which determine how expressions are evaluated when multiple operators are involved. Recognizing the natural order in which operations occur helps prevent logical errors and improve code clarity. You also discovered how parentheses can be used to enforce a specific evaluation order, providing better control over expression outcomes. Mastering these concepts equips you with the tools to write clear, precise, and bug-free code in Java.

Chapter Summary

- Java provides a variety of operators, including arithmetic, relational, logical, assignment, unary, ternary, and bitwise, each serving a specific purpose in expressions and program logic.

- Operators can be combined in a single statement, and understanding how they interact is essential for writing accurate and efficient code.

- Java follows a well-defined order of precedence, which determines the sequence in which operators are evaluated in compound expressions.

- Associativity defines how operators of the same precedence level are evaluated, typically from left to right or right to left.

- Using parentheses is the most effective way to clarify or override default precedence, ensuring that expressions behave as intended.

Quiz

1. Which of the following is an arithmetic operator in Java?

   a. &&
   b. +
   c. ==
   d. =

2. What does the == operator do in Java?

   a. Assigns a value
   b. Adds two numbers
   c. Compares two values for equality
   d. Checks memory address

3. Which of the following operators has the highest precedence?

   a. +
   b. *
   c. =
   d. &&

4. What is the output of this expression:
   10 + 5 * 2?

   a. 30
   b. 25
   c. 20
   d. 15

5. Which of the following is a logical operator in Java?

    a. ++

    b. ||

    c. >=

    d. %

6. What is the result of this ternary operation:
```
int x = (5 > 3) ? 10 : 20;?
```

    a. 5

    b. 3

    c. 10

    d. 20

7. What does the ++ operator do when placed after a variable (e.g., x++)?

    a. Increments and returns the new value

    b. Returns the original value, then increments

    c. Decrements the value

    d. Multiplies the value

8. Which operator is used for bitwise AND in Java?

    a. &&

    b. &

    c. |

    d. ^^

9. Which operator has right-to-left associativity?

   a. +
   b. *
   c. =
   d. <

10. What is the best way to ensure a specific order of operations in an expression?

    a. Use shorter expressions
    b. Add more operators
    c. Use parentheses
    d. Remove white space

Answers

1 – b	2 – c	3 – b	4 – c	5 – b
6 – c	7 – b	8 – b	9 – c	10 – c

Coding Task

Coding Task 1:

- Declare and initialize three int variables: a = 10, b = 5, and c = 2.
- Compute and print the result of the following expression: a + b * c - b / c.
- Demonstrate your understanding of operator precedence without using parentheses.
- Then rewrite the expression with parentheses to alter the result and print the new result. You have to figure out where to place the parentheses in the given equation in order to get the given output.

Expected Output:

```
Result without parentheses: 19
Result with parentheses: 7
```

Coding Task 2:

- Ask the user to enter two integer values.
- Use logical AND (&&) and logical OR (||) operators to:
- Check if both numbers are even
- Or if at least one of them is greater than 50
- Print appropriate messages based on the conditions.

Expected Output:

```
Enter first number: 24 <ENTER>
Enter second number: 55 <ENTER>
Both numbers are even: false
At least one number is greater than 50: true
```

Coding Task 3:

Requirements:

- Ask the user to input a test score (integer).
- Use a ternary operator to assign a result message:
- "Passed" if score is 75 or above
- "Failed" otherwise
- Print the assigned message.

Expected Output 1:

```
Enter score: 82 <ENTER>
Result: Passed
```

Expected Output 2:

```
Enter score: 71 <ENTER>
Result: Failed
```

Coding Task 4:

Requirements:

- Declare an integer variable `counter = 10`.
- Apply the following compound assignments in sequence:

```
counter += 5;
counter *= 2;
counter -= 4;
```

- Print the final value of the counter.

Expected Output:

```
Final value of counter: 26
```

Coding Task 5:

Requirements:

- Declare two integer variables: x = 6 and y = 3;
- Perform and print the results of the following bitwise operations:

```
x & y
x | y
x ^ y
```

- Include comments to explain what each result means in binary.

Expected Output:

```
x & y = 2 // 110 & 011 = 010
x | y = 7 // 110 | 011 = 111
x ^ y = 5 // 110 ^ 011 = 101
```

Practice More, Get Better!

Additional coding tasks for this chapter are available in the exclusive online resources that accompany this book.

CHAPTER **5**

Java Control Structures

Key Learning Objectives

- Use `if`, `if-else`, and `if-else-if` conditions to control the logical flow of your Java programs.
- Apply the `switch-case` statement effectively, including the use of `break` and `default cases`, as an alternative to complex `if` chains.
- Implement different types of loops — `while`, `do-while`, and `for` — to execute code repeatedly based on conditions.
- Use the `break` and `continue` statements to control loop execution flow.
- Understand and apply labelled `break` and labelled `continue` statements for nested loop control and complex flow scenarios.

Control structures are the backbone of decision-making and repetition in any programming language, and Java provides a rich set of tools for managing program flow. In this chapter, you will learn how to guide your program's behavior using conditional logic through `if`, `if-else`, and `switch-case` statements.

You'll explore various looping constructs such as `while`, `do-while`, and `for` loops, which allow sections of code to repeat based on dynamic conditions. In addition, you'll see how `break` and `continue` statements can be used to alter the flow of loops, and how labelled `breaks` and `continues` give you precise control over nested loop structures. Mastery of these control structures is essential for writing flexible, efficient, and readable Java programs that can adapt to different inputs and scenarios.

5.1 Introduction to Java Control Structures

To control the program flow based on certain conditions, logic, and flow, we need to use the Java control structures. In this chapter, we will discuss five of them: the `if`-condition, `switch-case`, `do-while`, `while`, and the `for` loop.

The **if**-condition is used to test the given condition and execute a statement block based on the result of the condition.

The `switch-case` statement is a branching statement that compares the value of a certain variable from a list of choices, which are called the case constants. If the value of the variable matches the case constant, then a group of statements will execute.

The `do-while` loop is used to continually execute a statement block while checking the result of the condition. The statement block will first execute then the condition will be checked, if it yields a `true` value, then it will again execute the statement block until it yields a `false` value, but in certain cases that the given condition gives out an initial value of false, the statement block will execute at least once because the condition checking is done at the end of the statement block.

The `while` statement, on the other hand, checks the condition first before executing the statement block. If the given condition yields a `true` value, then it executes the loop body, but if it yields a `false` value, then the entire while-statement block will be skipped.

The `for`-loop is also a looping construct and is ideal to use if you know the exact number of times you need to execute a statement block. Detailed discussion for each control structure is provided below.

5.2 The `if` Condition and Its Variants

5.2.1 The `if` Condition

The **if** condition is a conditional statement in Java that is used to test conditions and execute a specific statement block. Its general form is:

```
if (condition)
     statement;
else
     statement;
```

where the `statement` may either be a single statement or a compound statement (more than one statement). If a single statement is used, there is no need to put a begin and end brace ({ }). If a compound statement follows after the condition, it is necessary to enclose the statements in a begin and end brace ({ }). This is the general form of the **if** condition with a compound statement:

```
if (condition) {

    statement 1;
    . . .
    statement n;
}
else {

    statement 1;
    . . .
    statement n;
}
```

Where n is the number of statements. If the condition is `true`, then the statement block following the condition (normally called the if-block) will be executed. Otherwise, if the given condition returns a `false` value, the statement block following `else` (normally called the else-block) will be executed. The `else` block is optional. Here is an example of an **if** condition using a simple statement:

```
boolean sleepyHead = true;
if (sleepyHead)
    System.out.println ("I need more sleep");
else
    System.out.println ("I want to party");
```

The given condition should yield a `boolean` value, in this case a `true` value, and therefore the output will be

```
I need more sleep
```

Here is another example of an `if` condition:

Let's say you are receiving 1000 pesos for your weekly allowance this semester. But if you pass all your enrolled subjects this semester, you will be rewarded with an additional 500 pesos increase on your allowance next semester. So the code will look like this:

```
int weeklyAllowance = 1000;
int additionalAllowance = 500;
boolean passedAllSubjects = false;
if (passedAllSubjects) {
      // begin brace
      System.out.println("Your allowance next semester is " +
      (weeklyAllowance + additionalAllowance));
      System.out.println("Thanks mom.");
}    // end brace
else {
      // begin brace
      System.out.println("Your allowance next
                  semester is " + weeklyAllowance );
      System.out.println("Can I have more?");
}    // end brace
```

This will give us an output of:

```
Your allowance next semester is 1000
Can I have more?
```

Notice the *if-block* and the *else-block,* they are enclosed by the begin and end braces ({ }).

Let's take a look at this next program:

```
boolean willGraduate = true;                      //1
if (willGraduate) {

      System.out.println("Congratulations!");   //2
      System.out.println("Job hunting comes next...");
}
System.out.println("Learning never ends.");      //3
```

This program segment will give us an output of:

```
Congratulations!
Job hunting comes next...
Learning never ends.
```

But if statement 1 is declared as a `boolean` `willGraduate = false;` only statement 3 will be executed. With the absence of the `else`-block, the statement following the `if`-block, in this case statement 3, will be executed regardless of the result of the condition.

5.2.2 The Nested `if` Condition

A nested `if` condition is an `if` condition within another `if` condition. Try to analyze the given syntax:

```
if (condition) {

    // outer if block statements
    if (condition) {

    // inner if-block statements
    }
    else {

    // inner else-block statements
    }
}
else {

    // outer else block statements
    if (condition) {

    // inner if-block statements
    }
    else {

    // inner else-block statements
    }
}
```

As seen in the above case, adding white spaces (spaces, tabs, and enter keys) in your code will surely make it more readable.

The **outer-if-condition** is evaluated first, and then if it returns a `true` value, the **outer-if-block** will be executed, and within that scope, you will encounter the **inner-if-condition**. If the **inner-if-condition** also returns a `true` value, then the **inner-if-block** will also be executed. If any condition returns a `false` value, then it is expected that the corresponding `else` statement will be executed. Providing indentation within each of the `if` blocks and `else` blocks improves the readability of your code.

```java
public class Alarm {

    public static void main(String[] args) {

        int currentTemperature = 50;
        int upperLimit = 50;
        boolean danger = true;
        if (currentTemperature >= upperLimit) {        // 1

            if (danger) {                              // 2

                System.out.println("Sound the Alarm");   // 3
            }
            else {

                System.out.println("Turn up the cooler");
            }
        }
        else {

            System.out.println("Let's heat up");
        }
    }   // end psvm (public static void main)
}   // end class
```

In this example, statement 1 and 2 returns a `true` value; therefore, statement 3 will execute. But the more obvious question is this: How will I know which `else` statement is connected with which `if`?

And the answer is … the rule for matching an else with an if is that an else always refers to the nearest if, which is not associated with another else clause.

Consider the following:

```
if (currentTemperature >= upperLimit)              // 1
    if (danger)                                    // 2
        System.out.println("Sound the Alarm");
    else                                           // 3
        System.out.println("Turn up the cooler");
```

How will you know which else clause goes with which if statement? As the rule goes, *"an else always refers to the nearest if which is not associated with another else clause".* Therefore, the else clause goes with line 2.

Regardless of the indentation, the rule stays the same.

```
if (currentTemperature >= upperLimit)              // 1
    if (danger)                                    // 2
        System.out.println("Sound the Alarm");
    else                                           // 3
        System.out.println("Turn the cooler on");
```

Statement 3 still goes with statement 2. Once you have grouped them, the association may change, like in this example:

```
if (currentTemperature >= upperLimit) {            // 1

    if (danger)                                    // 2
        System.out.println("Sound the Alarm");
}
else                                               // 3
        System.out.println("Turn the cooler on");
```

Now the else statement goes with statement 1.

When the compiler sees an else statement, it pairs it with the closest preceding if statement that does not already have an associated `else`. This rule helps avoid ambiguity in nested conditional statements.

```java
int x = 5;
if (x > 10) {
    System.out.println("x is greater than 10");
}
if (x < 10) {
    System.out.println("x is less than 10");
}
else {
    System.out.println("x is equal to 10");
}
```

The second `if (x < 10)` is the nearest `if` to the `else`. The `else` pairs with `if (x < 10)` because the first `if (x > 10)` is already closed and does not affect the pairing. When x = 5, the output is: "`x is less than 10`" (from the second `if`) because the condition is `true`. The `else` is ignored because it only runs when `if (x < 10)` is `false`.

This rule is especially important when dealing with nested or complex conditional logic. If you don't explicitly use braces (`{ }`), it can become difficult to determine which `if` the `else` is paired with. To avoid confusion, it's a good practice to always use braces, even for single-statement blocks, or to use proper indentation.

```java
int y = 15;
if (y < 10)
    if (y > 5)
        System.out.println("y is between 6 and 9");
    else
        System.out.println("y is 10 or more");
```

The `else` pairs with the closest unmatched `if`, which is `if (y > 5)`.

When y = 15, the condition y < 10 is false, so the inner if and else are skipped entirely, and no output occurs.

By understanding this rule, you can write more predictable and accurate if-else constructs in Java.

5.2.3 The if - else - if Ladder

The if - else - if ladder looks like this:

```
if (condition) {

    statement/s;
}
else if (condition) {

    statement/s;
}
else if (condition) {

    statement/s;
    .

    .
}
else {

    statement/s;
}
```

The conditions are evaluated from top downward. The compiler tests each condition until a true condition is found. If a true condition is found, then the rest of the conditions will be bypassed. If there are no true conditions, then the else-block will be executed.

Here is an example of an **if** - **else** - **if** ladder:

```java
// Source File: GuessTheNumberGame.java
public class GuessTheNumberGame {

    public static void main(String[] args) {

        int magicNumber = 123;
        int guess = 100;
        if (guess == magicNumber) {

            System.out.println("*** Right ***");
            System.out.println(magicNumber +
                    " is the magic number");
        }
        else if (guess > magicNumber) {
            System.out.println("Wrong..Too High");
        }
        else {
            System.out.println("Wrong..Too Low");
        }
    }
}
```

5.3 The `switch-case` and Its Variants

5.3.1 The `switch-case` Statement

Switch is a multi-branch decision statement in Java that tests a list of constants. When a match is found, a statement block is executed. The general form of a switch statement is:

```
switch (controlVariable) {
        case constant1: statement sequence;
                        [break;]
        case constant2: statement sequence;
                        [break;]
        case constant3: statement sequence;
                        [break;]
                .
                .
        [default:                statement sequence;]
    }
```

where the default statement is executed if **no match** is
found. The default is optional and, if not present, no action
takes place if all matches fail. When a match is found, the
statement associated with that case is executed until the
break statement is reached or, in the case of the default
(or last case if no default is present), the end of the
switch statement is encountered. The break statement
is also optional. Without the break statement, the code
continues to execute the next case(s) even if they don't
match, this is known as the *fall-through* behavior. This can
lead to unintended outcomes if multiple case blocks are
executed when only one should be.

Refer to Table 5.1 to know the allowed Java data types that
can be used for the switch-case statement.

Table 5.1   **List of data types for the *switch-case* statement**

Allowed	byte, short, int, char, enum, String
Not Allowed	boolean, float, double, long, reference types

Here is a sample code that uses switch-case statements.

```java
// Source File: DisplayWordedValue.java
public class DisplayWordedValue {
    public static void main(String[] args) {
        byte number = 3;
        // short number = 3;
        // int number = 3;
        switch (number) {
            case 0: System.out.println("Zero"); break;
            case 1: System.out.println("One"); break;
            case 2: System.out.println("Two"); break;
            case 3: System.out.println("Three"); break;
            case 4: System.out.println("Four"); break;
            case 5: System.out.println("Five"); break;
            case 6: System.out.println("Six"); break;
            case 7: System.out.println("Seven"); break;
            case 8: System.out.println("Eight"); break;
            case 9: System.out.println("Nine"); break;
            default: System.out.println("out of range");
        }
    }
}
```

Notice that there are ten case choices to choose from. If the variable number has other values aside from 0 to 9, then the default statement is executed. In an event that all the case constant fails and the default statement is not present, then no statement will execute.

There are a few important things to know about the switch-case statement:

1. The switch differs from if in that the switch can only test for equality, whereas the if condition can evaluate a relational or logical expression.

   Using the if condition:

```
if (salary < 20000)                    // 1
        System.out.println("Underpaid");
if (salary == 20000)                   // 2
        System.out.println("Pay is ok");
if (salary > 20000)                    // 3
        System.out.println("Very good pay");
```

Using the `switch-case` statement:

```
switch (salary) {
        case 20000 : System.out.println ("Pay is ok");
        break;
}
```

Notice that only statement 2 can be converted to its `switch-case` counterpart.

2. No two `case` constants in the same `switch` can have identical values. A `switch` statement enclosed by an outer `switch` may have `case` constants that are the same.

Let us consider this:

```
char ch = 'a';
switch(ch) {
    // 1
    case 'a': System.out.println("Apple");
            break;
    // 2
    case 'A': System.out.println("Another Apple");
}
```

This example will compile and run properly with an output of:

```
Apple
```

Statement 1 and statement 2 are not identical. Let us remember that Java is case sensitive, therefore, characters 'a' and 'A' are not identical.

```
char ch = 'a';
switch(ch) {
    // 1
    case 'a': System.out.println("Apple");
            break;
    // 2
    case 'a': System.out.println("Another Apple");
}
```

An error during compilation will occur because the case constants in statements 1 and 2 are identical; it will give out an error message similar to this:

```
Letter.java:10: duplicate case label
        case 'a': System.out.println("Another Apple");
            ^
1 error
```

Identical case constants within different switches are allowable. Consider this next example:

```
char ch = 'a';
switch(ch) {                                        // 1

    case 'a': System.out.println("Apple");          // 2
            switch(ch) {                            // 3

                case 'a':
                    System.out.println("Another Apple"); // 4
            }
}
```

Examine the given code segment. This is legal because even though there were identical case constants, they belong to different switches. Statements 1 and 2 belong together, and statements 3 and 4 belong together. This will compile and will give us an output similar to this:

```
Apple
Another Apple
```

3. Only `byte`, `short`, `int`, `char`, `enum`, or `String` data types can be used for `switch-case` statements. Integral values must be within the range of their respective types. The `boolean`, `double`, `float`, `long`, and reference data types can not be used as `case` constants.

Cases That Have Common Statements

These are switch-case statements that have a common statement block but different case constants:

```
switch(letter) {
      case 'A': // this case has a common statement
      case 'a': System.out.println ("Apple");
            break;
      case 'B':
      case 'b': System.out.println ("Bike");
            break;
      case 'C':
      case 'c': System.out.println ("Cat");
            break;
      default : System.out.println ("Not an ABC character");
}
```

This sample code will test small and capital letters, but will have a common statement.

This routine illustrates two facets of the `switch` statement. First, you can have empty `case` statements. Second, if no `break` statement is present, execution will slide down to the next `case` statement.

Here is another program code that will show that the break statement is not always needed.

```java
// Source File: RoomForRent1.java
public class RoomForRent1 {
    public static void main(String[] args) {
        // room type numerical declaration
        int royalSuite = 1;
        int suite = 2;
        int juniorSuite = 3;
        int deluxe = 4;
        int roomType = suite;

switch(roomType) {
        case 1: System.out.println("Jacuzzi");
                System.out.println("Hair Blower");
                System.out.println("Water Bed");
                System.out.println("Cable TV");
                System.out.println("AirCon ");
                System.out.println("Shower");
                System.out.println("Bed");
                break;

        case 2: System.out.println("Hair Blower");
                System.out.println("Water Bed");
                System.out.println("Cable TV");
                System.out.println("AirCon ");
                System.out.println("Shower");
                System.out.println("Bed");
                break;

        case 3: System.out.println("Cable TV");
                System.out.println("AirCon ");
                System.out.println("Shower");
                System.out.println("Bed");
                break;

        case 4: System.out.println("AirCon ");
                System.out.println("Shower");
                System.out.println("Bed");
        }
    }
}
```

Some programmers tend to always use the break statement every time they use the switch-case statement. Let us now rewrite RoomForRent1.java to RoomForRent2.java. This time, let us remove the use of break statements for each case constant.

```java
// Source File: RoomForRent2.java
public class RoomForRent2 {
    public static void main(String[] args) {
            int royalSuite = 1;
            int suite = 2;
            int juniorSuite = 3;
            int deluxe = 4;
            int roomType = suite;

switch(roomType) {
                    case 1: System.out.println("Jacuzzi");
                    case 2: System.out.println("Hair Blower");
                            System.out.println("Water Bed");
                    case 3: System.out.println("Cable TV");
                    case 4: System.out.println("AirCon");
                            System.out.println("Shower");
                            System.out.println("Bed");
            }
    }
}
```

Now compare **RoomForRent1.java** and **RoomForRent2.java**, although both programs will have the same output, the coding style is very different. The output of both programs, once compiled and run, is:

```
Jacuzzi
Hair Blower
Water Bed
Cable TV
AirCon
Shower
Bed
```

In **RoomForRent1,** redundancy is evident, unlike in **RoomForRent2,** in which the repeated use of statements for each case constant is eliminated.

5.3.2 Strings and `switch-case`

Starting with Java 7, a new feature was introduced. You can now use String literal values in case statements. Consider the given snippet:

```
int result = 0;
switch(str.toLowerCase()) {
    case "one" : result = 1; break;
    case "two" : result = 2; break;
    case "three": result = 3;
}
return result;
```

This code snippet will only work for Java version 7 or higher, and will cause a compilation error if you use earlier versions.

5.3.3 Language Enhancements for Java 13 and Java 14

As the newer versions of Java are introduced, so are the new set of language features. In Java 13 and Java 14, there are several language enhancements introduced in `switch-case`. Originally a preview feature in Java 12, but was made permanent in Java 13 onwards.

If we wanted to return the number of days in a month, we could use the same structure that we have been using before Java 13.

```
switch (month.toUpperCase()) {
    case "JANUARY"    :
    case "MARCH"      :
```

```
    case "MAY"           :
    case "JULY"          :
    case "AUGUST"        :
    case "OCTOBER"       :
    case "DECEMBER"      : System.out.println(month +
                             " has 31 days."); break;

    case "APRIL"         :
    case "JUNE"          :
    case "SEPTEMBER"     :
    case "NOVEMBER"      : System.out.println(month +
                             " has 30 days."); break;
    case "FEBRUARY"      : System.out.println(month +
                             " has 28 / 29 days."); break;
    default              : System.out.println("Invalid Month");
}
```

In Java 13, the arrow (->) operator was introduced as a
new feature for `switch` statements. It simplifies the syntax,
allowing code to be cleaner and more expressive. With
this, cases can return values or execute multiple statements
without needing a `break` to prevent fall-through, which
reduces common errors and makes the code easier to read
and maintain.

```
    switch (month.toUpperCase()) {
        case "JANUARY", "MARCH", "MAY",
            "JULY", "AUGUST", "OCTOBER",
            "DECEMBER" -> System.out.println(month +
                            " has 31 days.");

        case "APRIL", "JUNE", "SEPTEMBER",
            "NOVEMBER" -> System.out.println(month +
                            " has 30 days.");

        case "FEBRUARY" -> System.out.println(month +
                            " has 28 / 29 days.");

        default -> System.out.println("Invalid Month");
    };
```

Using the arrow operator (->), you can also assign a value to a variable from a `switch-case` statement.

Before Java 13, we had to do this:

```java
int year = 2020;
int febNumberOfDays = year % 4 == 0 ? 29 : 28;
int numberOfDays;
String month = "January";

switch (month.toUpperCase()) {
    case "JANUARY"    :
    case "MARCH"      :
    case "MAY"        :
    case "JULY"       :
    case "AUGUST"     :
    case "OCTOBER"    :
    case "DECEMBER"   : numberOfDays = 31; break;
    case "APRIL"      :
    case "JUNE"       :
    case "SEPTEMBER"  :
    case "NOVEMBER"   : numberOfDays = 30; break;
    case "FEBRUARY"   : numberOfDays = febNumberOfDays;
                        break;
    default           : System.out.println("Invalid Month");
}
System.out.println("In the year " + year +
        " there are " + numberOfDays +
        " days on the month of " + month);
```

Java 13 onwards, we can now translate this to a new and shorter `switch-case` construct that uses the arrow operator and immediately assigns the result of the `switch-case` to a variable.

```
int year = 2020;
int febNumberOfDays = year % 4 == 0 ? 29 : 28;
int numberOfDays;
String month = "January";

numberOfDays = switch (month.toUpperCase()) {
        case "JANUARY", "MARCH", "MAY", "JULY",
             "AUGUST", "OCTOBER", "DECEMBER" -> 31;
        case "APRIL", "JUNE", "SEPTEMBER",
             "NOVEMBER" -> 30;
        case "FEBRUARY" -> febNumberOfDays;
        default -> 0;
};
System.out.println("In the year " + year +
            " there are " + numberOfDays +
            " days on the month of " + month);
```

Another way to use the arrow operator (->) is by placing it inside a `println()` method.

```
public static void numberToWords(int num) {
    System.out.println(
        switch (num) {
            case 1 -> "one";
            case 2 -> "two";
            case 3 -> "three";
            default-> "other number";
        }
    );
}
public static void main(String[] args) {
    numberToWords(2);
}
```

All these new language features for Java 13 are called "preview" features, which require an additional option during compilation and runtime. In compiling a Java source code with these new features inside an additional -enable-preview and -source 13 must be included as a compilation option, and -enable-preview for the runtime option.

To compile:

```
javac --enable-preview -source 13 SwitchUpdates.java
```

To run:

```
java --enable-preview SwitchUpdates
```

However, the compilation option `--enable-preview` `-source 13` and the runtime option `--enable-preview` are not required starting Java 14 and above, as they have been made a permanent feature.

5.4 The `while` Statement

Repeated action is one of the reasons why we need computers. When a large amount of data needs to be executed frequently, it is very convenient to have a control mechanism for frequent execution. This is why we have the `while` statement. It gives us control in executing a large number of instructions repeatedly.

The general form of the while statement is:

```
while (condition){
        statement block;
}
next statement;
```

Before the *statement block* is executed, the condition is first evaluated. If the condition returns a `true` value, then the *statement block* will be executed. But if the condition returned a `false` value, then the compiler will skip the statement block and will execute the statement following the sequence. Here is an example:

```
int sum = 0;
int i = 0;
```

```
while (i <= 10) {
      sum += i;
      ++i;
}
```

With this program segment, it will continually increment the value of *i* by 1 until the condition of the `while` statement returns false. The first time that the loop will execute the value of sum = 0 + 1, after the second time through the loop the value of sum is 1 + 2, then the third time, sum will be 2 + 3 and so on as long as the condition i <= 10 returns a `true` value.

5.5 The `do-while` Statement

The `do-while` statement is considered to be a variant of the while statement. Here is the general form:

```
do {
        statement block;
} while (condition);
next statement;
```

The statement block is first executed, and then the condition is evaluated. If the condition returned a `true` value, the first statement in the `do-while` loop will be executed again. The statement block will be executed continuously until the condition returns a `false` value.

Here is an example of a program segment that uses a do-while statement:

```
int sum = 0;
int i = 0;
do {
    sum += i;
    ++i;
} while (i <= 10);
```

As you can see, the statement block is executed first, then checks the condition. Unlike the `while` statement, Java checks the condition first, and if the condition is `true`, the *statement block* is executed.

The Difference Between the while and the do-while Statements

If the `do-while` statement is just a variant of the `while` statement, then what's the difference?

In the `while` statement, the condition is first checked before executing the statement block, unlike in the `do-while` you execute the statement first before testing the condition. In the `do-while` statement, the statement block will execute at least once regardless of the result of the given condition.

When working with `while` or `do-while` loops, always ensure the loop has a valid exit condition. Forgetting to update the loop variable or writing a condition that is always `true` can cause an *infinite loop*, which will make your program run endlessly and potentially crash your system or freeze your terminal.

Here's an example of what not to do:

```java
int counter = 1;

while (counter < 5) {
    System.out.println("Still running...");
    // Missing: counter should be incremented here!
}
```

In the example above, the condition `counter < 5` will always be `true` because counter is never updated inside the loop. This results in an *infinite loop*.

For best practices, always double-check that the loop will eventually reach a condition that becomes `false`.

5.6. The `for` Loop

A `for` loop allows a set of instructions to be performed until a certain condition is reached. The general form of the `for` loop is:

```
for (expr1; expr2; expr3) {
    statement block;
}
```

The **for** statement has three expressions: `expr1` initializes and/or declares the variable/s that will be used, `expr2` is the `boolean` expression that will determine if the loop will execute or not, and `expr3` increments or decrements the variable every time the loop is repeated. All three of these expressions are optional.

```
for (int i = 1; i <= 5; i++) {
    System.out.println("The value of i is: " + i);
}
```

In this program segment, i is initialized to 1. Since i is less than 5, `System.out.println()` is called, and i is incremented by 1. This process repeats until i is greater than 5, and at this point the loop terminates. In this example, i is the loop *control variable*, which is changed and checked each time the loop repeats.

The output would be:

```
The value of i is: 1
The value of i is: 2
The value of i is: 3
The value of i is: 4
The value of i is: 5
```

The three expressions in the `for` loop are optional. In the absence of the three expressions, two semicolons must remain inside the parentheses; this will give us an infinite loop.

```
for ( ; ; )
```

The only way to stop an infinite loop is by terminating the program abnormally, by pressing Control Break (CTRL + C).

5.7. The break Statement…Again

The break statement is not only used for switch-case, but it is also used for for-loops, do-while, and while statements. If the break statement is encountered inside any looping constructs, the rest of the statement block will be skipped, and the statement following the statement block will be executed. Here is an example:

```
for (int i = 1; i <= 5; i++) {

    if (i % 3 == 0) {                              // 1

        break;
    }
    System.out.println(i);                         // 2
}
System.out.println("Outside the loop");            // 3
```

The control variable i is initialized to 1 and is supposed to execute 5 times (from 1 to 5), but within the loop, there was an if condition in line 1 that tested the control variable i. When i becomes 3, line number 2 is skipped along with the rest of the loop, thus executing line 3, which is the next statement following the statement block. The output will therefore be:

```
1
2
Outside the loop
```

5.8. The `continue` Statement

The continue statement is used only for looping constructs such as `for`, `do-while`, and `while` loops. It allows you to prematurely terminate the current loop body and return the program control back to the beginning of the loop for a new iteration. Let us take a look at a similar example:

```
for (int i = 1; i <= 5; i++) {              // 1

    if (i % 3 == 0) {                       // 2

        continue;
    }
    System.out.println(i);                  // 3
}
System.out.println("Out of the loop");      // 4
```

In this example, the output will be:

```
1
2
4
5
Out of the loop
```

The control variable `i` is initialized to 1. Then the loop body is executed, thus printing the initial value of `i`, which is 1. The loop will count from 1 to 5, but within the `for` loop, an `if` condition is present. When `i` becomes equal to 3, the `continue` statement is executed, thus returning the program control back to statement number 1 in where `i` is once more incremented to 4, thus skipping statement number 2. When `i` becomes 5, the last value of `i`, which is 5, is printed, then incrementing it again to 6, which ends the loop, thus printing statement number 4.

The `break` and `continue` statements are used for all types of loops. The `break` statement, however, can also be used for `switch-case` statements. Refer to the table below.

Table 5.2	List of control structures for the *break* and *continue* statements

	if-else	switch-case	while	do-while	for
break	X	✔	✔	✔	✔
continue	X	X	✔	✔	✔

You can only use the break and continue statements within the if condition if the said condition is within a looping construct.

5.9. Labeled breaks and continues

Let's say that you have a nested loop like this:

```
for (i = 0; i < 5; i++) {
    for (j = 0; j < 5; j++) {
        break;                          // 1
        // inner implementation
    }
    // outer implementation              // 2
}
```

A break statement was encountered in statement 1 within the inner loop. This will allow you to break out of the inner loop and proceed with the execution to statement 2.

But what if you would like to break out not only from the inner loop but also out of the outer loop while being inside the inner loop? In this case, we are going to use the labeled break as shown below:

```
outerLoop:                              // 1
for (i = 0; i < 5; i++) {
    innerLoop:                          // 2
    for (j = 0; j < 5; j++) {
        break outerLoop;                // 3
```

```
            // inner implementation
      }
      // outer implementation                     // 4
   }
   // implementation outside the outer loop       // 5
```

In this example, statement 1 labels the outer `for` loop as `outerLoop` and statement 2 labels the inner `for` loop as `innerLoop`. The statement `break outerLoop` in statement 3 allows you to break out of the outermost loop; thus, once encountered, execution will go directly to statement 5.

If statement 3 is changed to `break` and not from its original example `break outerLoop`, this statement is the same as `break innerLoop`, which allows you to break out from the inner loop only, thus afterwards executing statement 4.

If we have labeled `breaks`, we also have labeled `continues`. The implementation is the same. Examine the following sample code:

```
   outerLoop:                                     // 1
   for (i = 0; i < 5; i++) {
         innerLoop:                               // 2
         for (j = 0; j < 5; j++) {
            continue outerLoop;                   // 3
            // inner implementation
         }
         // outer implementation                  // 4
   }
   // implementation outside the outer loop       // 5
```

In the inner loop, statement 3 is encountered, which allows you to continue the execution of the outer loop, but if statement 3 is replaced with `continue` or `continue innerLoop` (which is the same) will just skip other statements in the inner loop and proceed execution to statement 2. Here's a sample code snippet:

```
outer:
for (int i = 1; i <= 3; i++) {                    // 1

    inner:
    for (int j = 3; j >= 1; j--) {                // 2

        if (i == j)
            break outer;
        System.out.println(i + ", " + j);  // 3
    }
}
```

This snippet, when placed inside a valid Java source file, will print:

```
1, 3
1, 2
```

It will break the outer loop once the values of i and j become equal.

In this chapter, you learned how Java control structures govern the flow of execution in a program. You explored the use of conditional statements like if, if-else, nested if, and if-else-if to make decisions based on logical conditions. You also examined the switch-case statement as a structured alternative for handling multiple value checks, including all its new syntax in Java language updates. The chapter also introduced you to Java's core looping constructs — while, do-while, and for loops — that allow repeated execution of code blocks. Additionally, you learned how to interrupt or skip parts of loops using break and continue, and how labelled break and continue statements can manage the flow of nested loops. Mastering these control structures is essential for building responsive, logical, and dynamic programs in Java.

Chapter Summary

- Java control structures allow your program to make decisions and repeat tasks based on dynamic conditions.

- The `if`, `if-else`, and `if-else-if` statements enable the conditional execution of code blocks based on boolean expressions.

- The `switch-case` structure provides a cleaner alternative to long `if` chains, especially when checking a single variable against multiple values.

- Java supports three main types of loops — `while`, `do-while`, and `for` — each used for repeating a block of code under specific conditions.

- `break`, `continue`, and their labelled variants give fine-grained control over loop execution, especially in nested loop scenarios.

Quiz

1. Which of the following data types below is NOT allowed to be used in a `switch-case` construct?

   a. `byte`
   b. `boolean`
   c. `int`
   d. `short`

2. Given the snippet:

```
int num = 0;
do {
      System.out.print(num);
      num += 3;
}while (num <= 10);
```

   What will be the printed output?

   a. 0369
   b. 369
   c. 036912
   d. 36912

3. Given the code snippet:

```
int totalAttendees = 10;
String result;

if(totalAttendees <= 2)
    result = "couple";
else if (totalAttendees > 2 && totalAttendees < 5)
    result = "a few";
else if (totalAttendees <= 5)
    result = "several";
else
    result = "many";
System.out.println(result);
```

What gets printed?

a. couple

b. a few

c. several

d. many

4. Given the code snippet:

```
boolean a = false;
int b = 5;
if ( _____ && ++b >= 5)
    System.out.print("true");
else
    System.out.print("false");
```

Which of the following options, once placed in the blank, will print the value true as the output?

a. a

b. b

c. !a

d. !b

5. Given the snippet below:

```
int num = 1;
while (num <= 10) {

    if (num == 5)
        break;
    System.out.print(num++);
}
```

What is the output?

a. 1234

b. 2345

c. 0123

d. 01234

6. Given the code snippet:

```
for (int i = 1; i <= 10; i++) {

    if (i % 3 == 0)
        break;
    System.out.print(i);
}
```

What will be the output?

a. 12

b. 012

c. 12457810

d. 123

7. Given the code snippet:

```
for (int i = 0; i <= 6; i++) {
    if (i == 4)
        continue;
    System.out.print(i);
}
```

What will be the output?

a. 4
b. 12356
c. 012356
d. 0123

8. Assume that the given snippet below is within a valid Java source code:

```
int i;
for (i = 1; i <= 10; i++)
    if (i % 3 == 0)
        break;
    System.out.print(i);
```

What is the output?

a. 3
b. 12
c. 369
d. 12457810

9. Assume that the given snippet below is within a valid Java source code:

```
int i, j;
for (i = 0; i < 3; i++)
    for (j = 3; j > 1; j--)
        System.out.print(i * j);
```

What is the output?

a. 003264
b. 000321642
c. 000321642963
d. 321642

10. Assume that the given well-indented snippet below is within a valid Java source code:

```
int i = 3, j = 3;
while (i-- > 1) {
    while (j-- > 1) {
        System.out.print(j + "" + i);
    }
}
```

What is the output?

a. 2212
b. 22
c. 12
d. 221202

Answers

1 – b	2 – a	3 – d	4 – c	5 – a
6 – a	7 – c	8 – a	9 – a	10 – a

Coding Task

Coding Task 1:

Ask the user for his name to print, and how many times you want his name to be printed.

Your program's output should be as follows:

```
What is your name? Lawrence <ENTER>
How many times do you want me to print it? 5 <ENTER>
```

Output:

```
1. Lawrence
2. Lawrence
3. Lawrence
4. Lawrence
5. Lawrence
```

Coding Task 2:

Prompt the user to input two integer values, then print all the numbers from the first number up to the second number, including both numbers.

Coding Task 3:

Create a Java Program that will ask the user to input two positive integer numbers. Compute and display the product of the said numbers without using the multiplication ('*') operator. In your code, you are NOT allowed to use the multiplication '*' operator. Remember that multiplication is the process of repeated addition. If you were able to do this, try getting the integer quotient and the modulo (remainder) of the two numbers you entered.

Coding Task 4:

Write a Java program that prints all numbers from 1 to 50, but skips multiples of 3.

Expected Output:

```
1
2
4
5
7
...
47
49
50
(No multiples of 3)
```

Practice More, Get Better!

Additional coding tasks for this chapter are available in the exclusive online resources that accompany this book.

CHAPTER 6

String, StringBuffer, and StringBuilder

Key Learning Objectives

- Introduction to the `String` class and the `String` object
- The commonly used `String` methods
- The `StringBuffer` vs `StringBuilder` classes and their differences

In this chapter, we will explore the `String` Object, which represents a sequence of characters and is one of the most commonly used objects in Java. We'll dive into various `String` methods that allow manipulation and processing of string data, such as concatenation, comparison, and substring extraction. Additionally, we will compare the `StringBuffer` and `StringBuilder` classes, both of which provide mutable alternatives to `String` objects. While both are used to modify string content, `StringBuffer` is thread-safe and synchronized, whereas `StringBuilder` is faster but not synchronized, making it ideal for single-threaded environments.

6.1 The `String` Class

`Strings` are a representation of character values such as `"abc"`. Now, notice that we need to enclose these literal values inside a pair of double quotes. Enclosing the `String` literals using a pair of single quotes may work in other languages, but not in Java.

We have several ways to create a `String` object. We can either use one of the constructors provided by the `String` class in the API documentation or we can do a direct assignment.

Strings are constants; their values cannot be changed after they have been created, while **StringBuffers** and **StringBuilders** support mutable **Strings**, which basically means that they can be changed.

For example:

```
String str = "abc";
```

is equivalent to:

```
char data[] = {'a', 'b', 'c'};
String str = new String(data);
```

6.1.1 Uses of the String Data Type

The `String` data type is used for a string of characters such as names, addresses, phone numbers, and so on.

Example:

```
"Lawrence"
"Java Programming"
"1234567890"
```

6.1.2 String Position vs. Length

In Java, each character in a String has a position, also known as an index, which starts at 0 for the first character. This means the last character of the String will be at the position length - 1.

The length() method returns the total number of characters in the String, starting from 1 (not 0). This can sometimes confuse beginners because positions start from 0, but length starts counting from 1.

Let's use the name LAWRENCE as an example:

```
Index (Position):  0 1 2 3 4 5 6 7
Characters:        L A W R E N C E
Length Count:      1 2 3 4 5 6 7 8
```

- The first character 'L' is at position 0.
- The last character 'E' is at position 7, but it's the 8th character in the String.
- The length() of "LAWRENCE" is 8, but the highest valid index is 7.

The key points here are as follows:

- Position (index) starts at 0.
- Length starts counting at 1, and is equal to the number of characters in the String.
- The last valid position in a String is always length - 1.

Understanding these concepts is crucial for tasks such as substring extraction, character comparison, and iteration over a String. The indices help specify exact positions, while the length ensures you know the boundaries, preventing errors like StringIndexOutOfBoundsException.

In Java, spaces, blank characters, punctuation, and other special symbols are all treated as individual characters. This means they are part of the `String` and contribute to its length.

Example:

```
System.out.println("Congratulations! "
                    + " You passed this subject.");
```

The `String` inside `System.out.println()` is a `String` constant. In an output statement, it is possible to concatenate `String` constants and numbers using the `+` operator. The number is automatically converted to a `String` once you concatenate it to another `String` value.

Example:

```
int grade = 70;
System.out.println("Your grade is " + grade);
```

6.2 Commonly Used String Methods

The class `String` includes methods for examining individual characters of the sequence, for comparing strings, for searching strings, for extracting substrings, and for creating a copy of a `String` with all characters translated to uppercase or to lowercase. The commonly used `String` methods are:

- `substring()`
- `length()`
- `charAt()`
- `concat()`
- `replace()`
- `toLowerCase()`
- `toUpperCase()`
- `equals()`
- `equalsIgnoreCase()`
- `compareTo()`

- trim()
- split()

1. The substring() Method

It is used to extract a portion of a String object.

Example 1:

```
String country = "Philippines";
System.out.println(country.substring(3));
```

Output:

```
lippines
```

The substring() method in Java is used to extract a portion of a String starting from a specific index. For example, in the code

```
String country = "Philippines";
System.out.println(country.substring(3));
```

The method call country.substring(3) tells Java to begin extracting characters starting at index 3 and continue to the end of the String. Since Java uses zero-based indexing, index 3 corresponds to the character 'l' in "Philippines". Therefore, the output is "lippines", which includes all characters from the 'l' onward. This method is particularly useful when you want to remove or skip a certain number of characters at the beginning of a String or extract a specific part of it.

Example 2:

```
String country = "Philippines";
System.out.println(country.substring(0,3));
```

Output:

```
Phi
```

Characters are printed starting from position number 0 up to the number of the length specified.

Example 3:

```
String country = "Philippines";
System.out.println(country.substring(9, 12);
```

Output:

```
Error
```

Produces a `StringIndexOutOfBoundsException` since the word has character positions only from 0 to 10.

2. The `length()` Method

Provides the number of characters in the string.

Example 1:

```
String country = "Philippines";
System.out.println(country.length());
```

Output:

```
11
```

To find the last character of the string, we can use the `.length()` method together with the `substring()` method.

Example 2:

```
String country = "Philippines";
System.out.println(country.substring(country.length()-1));
```

Output:

```
s
```

3. The `charAt()` Method

It is used to find the character at any String position.

Example 1:

```
String country = "Philippines";
System.out.println(country.charAt(1));
```

Output:

```
h
```

You can also use the actual String value instead of the variable that holds the value.

Example 2:

```
String country = "Philippines";
System.out.println("Philippines".charAt(1));
```

Output:

```
h
```

Concatenation of Strings

The concatenation operator + can be used to join, or concatenate, string expressions.

Example 1:

```
String a = "abc";
String b = "def";
String c = a + c;
System.out.println(c);
System.out.println(c + "ghi");
```

Output:

```
abcdef
abcdefghi
```

4. The `concat()` Method

Aside from using the '+' operator, we can also use the `concat()` method to concatenate `Strings`. Both methods can be used to obtain the same result when joining two `Strings` together.

Example 1:

```
String a = "abc";
String b = "def";
String c = a.concat(b);
System.out.println(c);
System.out.println(c.concat( "ghi"));
```

Output:

```
abcdef
abcdefghi
```

5. The `replace()` method

Replacing characters in a `String`
Example:

```
String a = "Juan";
String b = a.replace('u', 'e');
System.out.println(a);
System.out.println(b);
```

Output:

```
Juan
Jean
```

6. The `toLowerCase()` and `toUpperCase()` Methods

Converting a string from uppercase to lowercase and vice versa.

```
String a = "Juan";
System.out.println(a.toUpperCase());
```

Output:

```
JUAN
```

```
String a = "Juan";
System.out.println(a.toLowerCase());
```

Output:

```
juan
```

7. The `equals()` Method

```
String a = "Juan";
String b = "Peter";
System.out.println(a.equals(b));
```

Output:

```
false
```

`a.equals(b)` is `true` if a and b are strings of the same length and they have the same characters in the same sequence.

```
String a = "Peter";
String b = "Peter";
System.out.println(a.equals(b));
Output: true
```

8. The `equalsIgnoreCase()` Method

```
String a = "Peter";
String b = "peter";
System.out.println(a.equals(b));
```

Output:

```
false
```

```
String a = "Peter";
String b = "peter";
System.out.println(a.equalsIgnoreCase(b));
```

Output:

```
true
```

9. The `compareTo()` Method

It is similar to equals, comparing Strings lexicographically. This allows the comparison of two Strings based on the order of characters, similar to a dictionary order. The term lexicographically refers to the way strings are compared based on the order of characters in the Unicode character set. This is similar to the alphabetical order in a dictionary, but it also considers the numeric and special characters since Java uses Unicode for character encoding.

```
String a = "Peter";
String b = "Peter";
System.out.println(a.compareTo(b));
```

Output:

```
0
```

- If a and b are equal, the value is 0
- If a is less than b, the value is negative
- If a comes after b, the value is positive

The method compares each character one by one from the beginning of the strings, using the Unicode values to determine which comes first. If a character in one string is greater than the corresponding character in the other, it will return a positive value. If they are equal, the comparison continues to the next character. If all characters match, the method returns zero.

10. The `trim()` Method

It is used to remove white spaces

```
String a = " Lawrence ";
System.out.println(a);
System.out.println(a.trim( ));
```

Output:

```
Lawrence
Lawrence
```

11. The `split()` Method

Splits this `String` around matches of the given tokens.

```
String str = "aaa:bbb:ccc";
String[] results = str.split(":");
for (String r : results) {
        System.out.println(r);
}
// this type of for-loop is known as the enhanced for loop
// which will be discussed in the next chapter on Arrays.
```

Output:

```
aaa
bbb
ccc
```

6.2.1 Text Blocks

Text blocks are new features introduced as a preview feature in Java 13 and Java 14. It allows the grouping of several `String` values together in different lines to be grouped by a fat delimiter composed of three double-quotes (`"""`).

Fat delimiters (`"""`) are used to allow double quote (") characters to appear unescaped. It also distinguishes a text block from a String literal. Text blocks are multi-line `String` literals that prevent the need for most escape sequences and format the `String` values automatically for easy formatting.

Consider the following code snippet:

```
5       String str1 = """
6               Hello
7               Aloha
8               Hi
9               """;
10      String str2 = "Hello\nAloha\nHi\n";
11
12      System.out.println("str1: " + str1);
```

```
13        System.out.println("str2: " + str2);
14
15        System.out.println("Compare str1 and str2: "
16                     + str1.equals(str1));
```

Output:

```
str1: Hello
Aloha
Hi

str2: Hello
Aloha

Hi

Compare str1 and str2: true
```

Lines 5 to 9 show the use of text blocks. The values of str1 and str2 when printed will produce the same output, and compared in lines 15 and 16, they will give you a true value.

Since text blocks are only "preview" features in Java 13 and 14, the compiler will require a compilation option --enable-preview to allow the compiler to access the preview feature and followed by -source 13 to specify the compiler's version.

Assuming the code snippet is inside a valid Java source code named TextBlock.java this is how you compile:

```
javac --enable-preview -source 13 TextBlocks.java
```

After a successful compilation of the Java source code, a virtual machine (VM) option --enable-preview is also required. To run, you have to type this command:

```
java --enable-preview TextBlocks
```

Starting Java 15 and above, you won't need the compilation option --enable-preview -source 13 and the runtime option --enable-preview anymore.

6.3 The `StringBuffer` and `StringBuilder` Classes

6.3.1 `StringBuffer`

`StringBuffer` is a mutable sequence of characters that allows modifications, unlike regular `String` objects. It can change its length and content through various methods, making it flexible for handling dynamic text. Additionally, `StringBuffer` is thread-safe, ensuring that multiple threads can work with it without causing synchronization issues.

`StringBuffers` are safe for use by multiple threads. The methods are synchronized where necessary so that all the operations on any particular instance behave as if they occur in some serial order that is consistent with the order of the method calls made by each of the individual threads involved.

The principal operations on a `StringBuffer` are the append and `insert` methods, which are overloaded so as to accept data of any type. Each effectively converts a given expression to a `String` and then `appends` or `inserts` the characters of that `String` to the `StringBuffer`. The append method always adds these characters at the end of the buffer; the `insert` method adds the characters at a specified point.

The `append()` method belongs to both the `StringBuffer` and `StringBuilder` classes, while the `concat()` method belongs to the `String` class.

6.3.2 `StringBuilder`

`StringBuilder` is a mutable sequence of characters. This class provides an API compatible with `StringBuffer`, but with no guarantee of synchronization. This class is designed for use as a drop-in replacement for `StringBuffer` in places where the `StringBuffer` was being used by a single thread (as is generally the case). Where possible, it is recommended that this class be used in preference to `StringBuffer` as it will be faster under most implementations.

The principal operations on a `StringBuilder` are the append and insert methods, as well, which are also overloaded so as to accept data of any type. Each effectively converts a given expression to a `String` and then appends or inserts the characters of that `String` to the `StringBuilder`. The append method always adds these characters at the end of the builder, same as `StringBuffer`; the insert method adds the characters at a specified point, also the same as `StringBuffer`.

6.3.3 The `append()` and the `insert()` Methods of the `StringBuffer` and `StringBuilder` Classes

Example1:

```
StringBuffer sb = new StringBuffer("abc");
sb.append("def");
System.out.println(sb);
```

Output:

```
abcdef
```

Example2:

```
StringBuffer sb = new StringBuffer("abc");
sb.insert(1, "def");
System.out.println(sb);
```

Output:

```
adefbc
```

These methods will have the same effect on both `StringBuffer` and `StringBuilder` objects.

To get the complete list of methods for `String`, `StringBuffer`, and `StringBuilder` classes, it is still best to look them up in the Java API Documentation.

Chapter Summary

In Java, `String`, `StringBuffer`, and `StringBuilder` are classes used to work with sequences of characters. Here are the common things among these three classes:

- All three classes belong to the `java.lang` package, which means they are automatically imported into every Java program.

- They are used to create and manipulate sequences of characters (strings).

- All three classes implement the `CharSequence` interface, which means they provide a standard way to access a sequence of characters.

- They all provide methods for basic string operations such as:

  - Length: `length()`
  - Character access: `charAt(int index)`
  - Substring extraction: `substring(int beginIndex, int endIndex)`

The Differences are as follows:

- `String` is immutable: Once a `String` object is created, it cannot be changed. Any modification to a `String` results in the creation of a new `String` object.

- `StringBuffer` and `StringBuilder` are mutable: They can be modified after creation without creating new objects. This makes them more efficient for scenarios where frequent modifications to the string are required.

- `String` concatenation is done using the `+` operator or the `concat()` method, which results in the creation of a new `String` object.

- `String` Text block was also introduced in Java 13 and 14, which uses fat delimiters (`" " "`) triple double quotes.

- As for both `StringBuffer` and `StringBuilder` classes, they provide methods like `append()` and `insert()` to modify the existing string, making concatenation more efficient.

- `StringBuffer` is thread-safe: All its methods are synchronized, which makes it safe for use by multiple threads, but can be slower due to the overhead of synchronization.

- `StringBuilder` is not thread-safe.

- `String` is immutable and thus inherently thread-safe.

- `StringBuilder` is not synchronized and should be used in single-threaded contexts.

Quiz

1. **Given two Strings:**

```
String s1 = new String("I love ");
String s2 = new String("Java Programming");
```

Which statement below will NOT produce an output of:

```
I love Java Programming
```

a. System.out.println(s1 + s2);
b. System.out.println(s1 + "" + s2);
c. System.out.println("s1" + "s2");
d. System.out.println(s1.concat(s2));

2. **Given the String declarations:**

```
String s1 = new String("JAVA");
String s2 = new String("java");
```

Which of the following statements below will give an output of true?

a. System.out.println(s1 == s2);
b. System.out.println(s1.equals(s2));
c. System.out.println(s1.toUpperCase().equals(s2));
d. System.out.println(s1.equalsIgnoreCase(s2));

3. **Given the String declaration:**

```
String str = "Java";
```

What method should we use to print the output?

JAVA

  a. `System.out.println(str.toUpperCase());`
  b. `System.out.println(str.UpperCase());`
  c. `System.out.println(str.toCapitalLetters());`
  d. `System.out.println(s.toUpperCase());`

4. **Which of the following is NOT TRUE about a String?**

  a. In the Java programming language, `Strings` are objects.

  b. `Strings` are sequences of characters enclosed in a pair of single quotes (' ').

  c. `Strings` are widely used in Java programming.

  d. `Strings` are a sequence of characters enclosed in a pair of double quotes (" ").

5. **Which of the following is NOT TRUE?**

  a. `String`, `StringBuffer`, and `StringBuilder` are the same set of

  b. `String` objects are immutable.

  c. `StringBuffer` and `StringBuilder` have identical sets of methods.

  d. `StringBuffer` and `StringBuilder` are mutable versions of the `String` object.

6. What symbol do you use to concatenate String values?

   a. =
   b. +
   c. #
   d. $

7. Which of the following statements below will cause an error in storing the value "I love coding" in the variable String str?

   a. `String str = I love coding;`
   b. `String str = new String("I love coding");`
   c. `String str = new String(new StringBuffer("I love coding"));`
   d. `String str = new String(new StringBuilder("I love coding"));`

8. Given the declaration:

   `String s = "Java";`

   How do we get the first character of a String s?

   a. s.atChar(1)
   b. s.atChar(0)
   c. s.charAt(1)
   d. s.charAt(0)

9. Given the code declaration:

```
StringBuffer sb = new StringBuffer("java");
```

Which of the following statements written independently WILL NOT print the output "java" (without the double quotes)? Use the Java API Documentation to look at the **reverse()** method in the **StringBuffer** class.

a. `System.out.println(sb.reverse().reverse().reverse());`

b. `System.out.println(sb.reverse().reverse().reverse().reverse());`

c. `System.out.println(sb.substring(0));`

d. `System.out.println(sb.substring(0, sb.length()));`

10. Given the code snippet:

```
String s1 = "I love";
String s2 = "Java ";
String s3 = "Coding";
System.out.println(s1.indexOf('o') + s2.indexOf('a') +
s3.indexOf('l'));
```

Using the Java API documentation, look at the indexOf() method in the String class. What will be the output of the given code snippet?

a. 3
b. 5
c. 7
d. 10

Answers

1 – c	2 – d	3 – a	4 – b	5 – a
6 – b	7 – a	8 – d	9 – a	10 – a

Coding Task

Coding Task 1:

Create a Java Program that will ask the user to enter their full name -- their first name followed by a space, then their last name. For simplicity, let us assume that a person will only have one first name and one last name. Once the full name is accepted, display the full name using a different format. The new format should be <last name>, <comma and space> <first name>.

Sample Output 1:

Enter full name:

```
Steve Rogers
```

New Format:

```
Rogers, Steve
```

Sample Output 2:

Enter full name:

```
Peter Parker
```

New Format:

```
Parker, Peter
```

Sample Output 3:

Enter full name:

Tony Stark

New Format:

Stark, Tony

Coding Task 2:

Write a Java program that takes two strings as input and checks if the input string is a palindrome. A string is a palindrome if it reads the same backward as forward. For example, "radar" and "level" are palindromes.

Coding Task 3:

Create a Java program that will ask the user to enter a String value. Determine and print the following:

- original input string
- last character of the String
- String length
- type of character (last character) - is it a vowel, a consonant, a digit, or a symbol?

Sample IO 1:

```
Enter a String value: I love Java<ENTER>
String: I love Java
Last Character: a
String length: 11
type of last char: vowel
```

Sample IO 2:

```
Enter a String value: C++ <ENTER>
String: C++
Last Character: +
String length: 3
type of last char: symbol
```

Note:

- The following are vowels: aAeEiIioOuU
- The following are the consonants: Letters that are not vowels
- The following are the digits: 0123456789
- The symbols are the characters that are NOT vowels, not consonants, and not digits

Practice More, Get Better!

Additional coding tasks for this chapter are available in the exclusive online resources that accompany this book.

CHAPTER 7
Arrays

Key Learning Objectives

- Introduction to arrays and their initial values upon creation
- Array Limits
- The Enhanced for loop
- Copying Arrays
- Command Line Arguments
- Array of Arrays (Two-dimensional Arrays)
- Non-Rectangular Arrays

In this chapter, we will dive into the very basic data structure in Java called arrays, exploring their versatility in managing collections of data. You'll learn about the various ways arrays can be used, from their basic creation to handling more complex forms like multi-dimensional arrays. We will cover best practices for working with arrays, including how to manipulate them efficiently and how they can interact with other elements of a Java program, such as command line arguments. Additionally, you'll understand how Java provides different approaches to iterate through arrays and deal with more advanced configurations like non-rectangular arrays. This will deepen your understanding of how arrays operate within the Java.

7.1 Introduction to Arrays

An array is a data structure in Java that is used to group common data types together. It is normally a homogeneous collection, which means that the data type of one element is the same data type of the other elements. It has a fixed size, and once the size has been set, it cannot be changed to accommodate other

Let's understand arrays with the help of an example. Let's say your instructor gave you five short quizzes for your midterms, instead of declaring them as:

```
int quiz1, quiz2, quiz3, quiz4, quiz5;
```

You may want to declare them as:

```
int[] quiz = new int[5];
```

This means that you are declaring and creating an array of quizzes of type integers that can have 5 integer values. Let us now determine the parts of the given array:

data type

```
int[] quiz;
```

array name

Sometimes you might need more than one array. You can use the following statement to declare multiple arrays in a single line:

```
int quiz[], seatwork[];
```

This is also equivalent to:

```
int[] quiz, seatwork; // preferred way to write arrays
```

Once the [] notation follows the data type declaration, all variables in the declaration are arrays; otherwise, the [] must follow after each variable.

You can declare arrays of any type, either a primitive data type or a reference data type. Arrays in Java are treated as objects. Therefore, we can construct our arrays by using the new keyword.

```
quiz = new int[5];      // array having 5 elements
seatwork = new int[7];  // array having 7 elements
```

You have now created an array of quizzes and an array of seatwork of type integers, having 5 and 7 elements respectively.

Array declaration and array creation can also be done in one statement:

```
int[] quiz = new int[5];
int[] seatwork = new int[7];
```

The Java programming language also allows the creation of arrays with initial values:

```
String names[] = {         // Array declaration
    "Lawrence",            // 1st element
    "Michelle",            // 2nd element
    "Danielle",            // 3rd element
    "Bernice"              // 4th element
};
```

Since Strings are objects, you can also declare them this way:

```
String names[] = {

    new String ("Lawrence"),
    new String ("Michelle "),
```

```
            new String ("Danielle "),
            new String ("Bernice ")
    };
```

Another example is the declaration and initialization of an array of `int`.

```
    int[] quizzes = {90, 100, 80, 70, 95};
```

Arrays have initial values upon creation.

Upon the creation of arrays, initial values are automatically assigned to them. Figure 7.1 shows the lists of data types with their initial values.

Figure 7.1 List of default values per data type

Variable	Value
byte	0
short	0
int	0
long	0L
float	0.0F
double	0.0D
char	'\u0000'
boolean	false
All reference types	null

Let's take a look at this example:

```
1    // ArraySample.java
2    public class ArraySample {
3
4        public static void main(String[] args) {
5
6            int[] intArray = new int[5];
7            for (int i = 0; i < intArray.length; i++)
8                System.out.println("The value of intArray[ "
9                        + i + " ] = " + intArray[i]);
10       }
```

```
11  }
```

Take a look at line 6. An array of integers was created, but the array was not initialized. Nevertheless, since it is an array of integers, a value of zero will be assigned to each element because zero (0) is the default value of each element of an array of int. As the code loops through the for loop body, it will give us an output of:

```
The value of intArray[ 0 ] = 0
The value of intArray[ 1 ] = 0
The value of intArray[ 2 ] = 0
The value of intArray[ 3 ] = 0
The value of intArray[ 4 ] = 0
```

Why did we have 0's as the values of the array intArray? This is because all arrays are automatically initialized upon creation.

7.2 Array Limits

All arrays begin with index 0. Let's take a look at this example:

```
String[] coffee = {
    "Barako",
    "Espresso",
    "Java",
    "Mocha chino"
};
```

The code snippet declares and initializes a one-dimensional array of String objects named coffee, which contains a list of coffee names. In Java, arrays are used to store multiple values of the same data type in a single variable. Here, the array coffee is initialized with four string elements: "Barako", "Espresso", "Java", and "Mocha chino".

Each element is automatically assigned an index starting from 0, meaning "Barako" is at index 0, "Espresso" at index 1, and so on.

This type of array is useful for storing and accessing a fixed set of related data items, such as menu options or product names, using indexed access within a loop or conditional structure.

Figure 7.2 List of *String* values per array index

```
coffee[]
```

"Barako"	0
"Espresso"	1
"Java"	2
"Mocha chino"	3

index

The index of the array coffee[] starts with 0 and ends with 3. So if you want to access Java, you would do it like this:

```
System.out.println ("I love " + coffee[2]);
```

This will give you an output like this:

```
I love Java
```

How do you access the last element of your array without knowing the exact number of elements in your array? Since arrays in Java are objects, they have a length attribute that returns the actual length of the array.

In Java, .length is a property used in arrays to determine the number of elements. It provides the size of the array, meaning how many slots it contains, regardless of whether those slots hold meaningful data. This is particularly helpful when working with arrays, as their size is fixed upon creation and cannot change dynamically.

Here's an example of how `.length` is used:

```
String[] coffee = {"Barako", "Espresso",
                   "Java", "Mocha chino"};
System.out.println("Number of coffee I had for the day: "
                   + coffee.length);
```

Output:

```
Number of coffees I had for the day: 4
```

In this example, .length returns 4 because there are four elements in the numbers array.

You can access the last element of the array `coffee` in the following way:

```
System.out.println ("My last coffee for the day is a "
                   + coffee[coffee.length-1]);
```

The output will be like this:

```
My last coffee for the day was a Mocha chino
```

`coffee.length` returns the number of elements in the array `coffee`, which is `4`. Therefore, we need to use `coffee.length-1` to access the last element of the array `coffee`. Without the `-1`, it will throw an `ArrayIndexOutOfBoundsException`. It means you are attempting to access an element that is beyond the array bounds, in this case, beyond `0` to `3`.

But how am I going to print all the elements of the array coffee?

That's easy. You can use a for loop or any type of loop to do it for you.

```
System.out.println ("The coffee lovers' choices are: ");
for (int i = 0; i < coffee.length; i++) {

    System.out.println (coffee[i]);
}
```

The output would be like this:

```
The coffee lovers' choices are:
Barako
Espresso
Java
Mocha chino
```

Using an integer variable i as an index, you can access all the elements of the array coffee from the first element until the last element coffee.length-1.

Now drink up and enjoy your coffee!

7.3 The Enhanced For Loop

The enhanced for loop in Java, also called the *"for-each"* loop, provides a simplified way to iterate over elements in a collection, array, or similar data structure. Its syntax is structured to eliminate the need for managing an index variable manually. Here's the breakdown of its syntax:

```
for (dataType element : array) {
    // Code block to process each element
}
```

The for loop created in the previous example can be rewritten this way:

```
11   String[] coffee = {
12        "Barako",
13        "Espresso",
14        "Java",
15        "Mocha chino"
16   };
17
18   System.out.println ("The coffee lovers' choices are: ");
19
20   for (String c : coffee) {
```

```
21        System.out.println (c);
22    }
```

In this example, `String c` takes on each value in the `coffee` array one at a time, and the loop body processes each value without requiring explicit indexing like in a traditional for loop.

The enhanced for loop was introduced in Java SE version 5, also called the `for-each` loop. The enhanced for loop was primarily created for `Collections`, which is another data type, but can also be used for arrays. Based on my experience, the enhanced for loop runs faster in most cases. We will discuss the `Collections` framework in the next volume of this book, but for now, our focus is on arrays.

The noticeable difference between the two is that in the traditional for loop, you can freely access the control variable (usually it's the variable `i`). But in the enhanced for loop, you cannot access your control variable.

Secondly, using the traditional for loop, you can iterate over the array (or over the `Collections`) from the first element down to the last and in reverse. In the enhanced for loop, you could only iterate through your array from the first element down to the last. A reverse iteration is just not possible.

7.4 Copying Arrays

If you need to put the elements of one array into another array, there's a convenient method for this. We can use the `System.arraycopy()` method.

The `System.arraycopy()` method in Java is a utility provided by the `System` class to copy elements from one array to another efficiently. It allows precise control over which elements are copied and where they are placed in the destination array.

Here's how its syntax works:

```
System.arraycopy(sourceArray, sourcePosition,
            destinationArray, destinationPosition, length);
```

- `sourceArray` is the array from which elements will be copied.
- `sourcePosition` is the starting index in the source array for copying.
- `destinationArray` is the array where elements will be pasted.
- `destinationPosition` is the starting index in the destination array where the copied elements will be placed.
- `Length` refers to the number of elements to copy.

Here's an example:

```
1    // ArrayCopyExample.java
2    public class ArrayCopyExample {
3
4        public static void main(String[] args) {
5
6            int[] orig = {1, 2, 3, 4, 5};
7            int[] temp = {10, 9, 8, 7, 6, 5, 4, 3, 2, 1};
8            System.arraycopy(orig, 0, temp, 0, orig.length);
9            orig = temp;
10           temp = null;
11           System.out.println("Printing the NEW array:");
12           for (int num : orig) {
13
14               System.out.print(num + "\t");
15           }
16       }
17   }
```

Once compiled and run, you will have the following output:

```
Printing the NEW array:
1   2   3   4   5   5   4   3   2   1
```

In line 7, `System.arraycopy(orig, 0, temp, 0, orig.length);` we need to pass five parameters to the `System.arraycopy()` method.

The first parameter is the original array, followed by the starting point of the source array, then the third parameter is the destination array, the fourth argument is the starting point of the destination array where you will start putting the copied elements, and the last argument is the number of elements to be copied.

7.5 Command Line Arguments

Command-line arguments in Java are particularly useful in scenarios where you want to provide input to a program at the time of its execution, without relying on hardcoded values or user interaction during runtime. They make programs flexible and adaptable, especially in automation and scripting tasks.

Imagine you are creating a Java program to accept inputs from the command line and print them afterwards.

In your `main` method, you have the following method signature:

```
public static void main(String[] args)
```

Some of you may ask, what is the **String[] args** for? It is Java's way to accept input via the command line.

Consider this first example:

```
1    // CommandLineArgs1.java
2    public class CommandLineArgs1 {
```

```
3
4          public static void main(String[] args) {
5
6              System.out.println(args[0]);
7              System.out.println(args[1]);
8              System.out.println(args[2]);
9          }
10  }
```

After compiling it, you can run it by providing command line arguments like this:

```
java CommandLineArgs1 one "two two" three
```

The Strings that come after the file name are command line arguments that are passed to the main method's array of `String` parameters. And each `String` is an element of the `args[]` array. You just need to separate each `String` with a space. But if you would like to include the space inside the `String`, you can enclose it with a pair of double quotes, just like what we did with this argument "*two two*". After execution, you will have the following output:

```
one
two two
three
```

What problem do you see in this example?

What if I would like to pass fewer than three arguments? Or say, pass more than three arguments?

```
java CommandLineArgs1 one "two two" three four five
```

You will have the same output:

```
one
two two
three
```

Your code is not that dynamic when it comes to displaying the number of elements in your command line. It does not accommodate other `String` values aside from the first three elements.

The number of argument lists is not dynamically accepted. We need to rewrite our code in a way that it can accept any number of elements that are passed via the command line:

```
1   // CommandLineArgs2.java
2   public class CommandLineArgs2 {
3       public static void main(String[] args) {
4           for (int i = 0; i < args.length; i++) {
5               System.out.println(args[i]);
6           }
7       }
8   }
```

Using `args.length` will allow you to access the size of the array, and by using it in a for loop, you can write a loop that will iterate from the first element down to the last.

But with the use of the enhanced for loop, it can also be rewritten this way.

```
1   // CommandLineArgs3.java
2   public class CommandLineArgs3 {
3       public static void main(String[] args) {
4           for (String arg : args) {
5               System.out.println(arg);
6           }
7       }
8   }
```

In this example, we must remember that when we pass arguments via the command line, we are passing `String` values, even if we pass integers or other data types. As a rule, all argument values passed via the command line are Strings because your `main` method can only accept an array of `String` values.

So, let's say we would like to pass integer values via the command line and then compute the sum and the average of the integer values. How do we do this?

Consider this code:

```
1    // CommandLineArgs4.java
2    public class CommandLineArgs4 {
3
4        public static void main(String[] args) {
5
6            int sum = 0;
7            for (String arg : args) {
8
9                sum += Integer.parseInt(arg);
10           }
11       System.out.println("Sum: " + sum);
12       System.out.println("Ave: " +
                    (double)sum / args.length);
13       }
14   }
```

When we compile and run this code with the following command line values, you will have the following output:

```
java CommandLineArgs4 1 22 3 4 5 6 7

Sum: 48
Ave: 6.857142857142857
```

As you can see in line 8, we converted the String parameter value to its integer equivalent by using the method from the Integer class **Integer.parseInt(arg)**. After the String value has been parsed, it can now be used for any mathematical operation, including addition.

7.6 Array of Arrays (Two-Dimensional Arrays)

A two-dimensional array in Java is like a table with rows and columns. You can think of it as an *array of arrays*. Each element in a two-dimensional array is accessed using two indices: one for the row and one for the column. You can have a rectangular "normal" two-dimensional array or a non-rectangular array.

7.6.1 Rectangular Two-Dimensional Arrays

Let's first take a look at the "normal" two-dimensional array. Consider this example:

```
int[][] numbers = {
        {10, 20, 30},
        {40, 50, 60}
};
```

In this example:

- `numbers[0][0]` refers to 10 – This is the element in row 0, column 0.
- `numbers[0][1]` refers to 20 – This is the element in row 0, column 1.
- `numbers[0][2]` refers to 30 – This is the element in row 0, column 2.
- `numbers[1][0]` refers to 40 – This is the element in row 1, column 0.
- `numbers[1][1]` refers to 50 – This is the element in row 1, column 1.
- `numbers[1][2]` refers to 60 – This is the element in row 1, column 2.

You can visualize the array like this:

Row 0 → [10] [20] [30]

Row 1 → [40] [50] [60]

Each element is accessed by its row index, followed by its column index, using the syntax:

`numbers[row][column].`

Just remember that array indices will always start with 0, even if it is a two-dimensional array.

Here are other practical examples when we can use two-dimensional arrays:

1. **Spreadsheets or Tables**

   Think of a program like Microsoft Excel or Google Sheets. Each cell in a spreadsheet can be identified by a row and a column. Similarly, a two-dimensional array lets you store and access data using two indices.

   Example:

```
String[][] grades = {
    {"Matthew", "85"},
    {"Mark", "92"},
    {"Luke", "78"}
};
```

   - grades[0][0] is "Matthew" (row 0, column 0)
   - grades[0][1] is "85" (row 0, column 1)

   This is useful when storing student names and their scores, or any data structured in rows and columns.

2. **Game Boards (e.g., Chess, Tic-Tac-Toe)**

   Games that involve grids are a perfect use case for 2D arrays. Each square on a chessboard, for instance, can be represented using a row and column.

   Example:

```
char[][] ticTacToe = {
    {'X', 'O', 'X'},
    {'O', 'X', 'O'},
    {' ', 'X', ' '}
};
```

You can easily check for a winner by scanning across rows, columns, or diagonals.

3. Images or Pixels

In digital images, each pixel can be thought of as a tiny square on a grid with a color value. You can represent this with a 2D array where each cell holds a color code or intensity level.

Example:

```
int[][] grayscaleImage = {
    {255, 128, 0},
    {64, 128, 192}
};
```

This can be used for image processing, filters, or computer vision tasks where you manipulate pixel data.

4. Seating Charts

In classrooms, theaters, or airplanes, seats are arranged in rows and columns. A 2D array can track which seats are occupied or available.

Example:

```
// 3 rows,4 seats per row
boolean[][] seats = new boolean[3][4];

// Seat in row 0, column 1 is taken
seats[0][1] = true;
```

This allows your program to manage reservations or availability efficiently.

A two-dimensional array is a versatile structure for modeling real-world layouts where data is arranged in rows and columns. It makes accessing, modifying, and organizing this kind of data much more logical and efficient in code. For Java beginners, mastering 2D arrays opens the door to more complex problem-solving and practical programming projects.

You can also create and declare a two-dimensional array with default values.

```
int[][] arr2d = new int[3][4];
```

We will use a memory diagram to visualize how the array is structured.

Figure 7.3 Two-dimensional array memory allocation

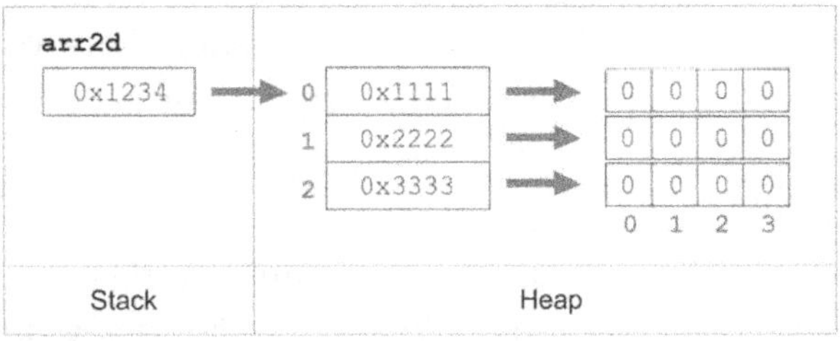

All elements are initialized to zero (0) since it is the default value of an `int`.

Declaring and initializing a multidimensional array is also possible this way:

```
int[][] arr2d = {
        {1,2,3,4},
        {2,4,6,8},
        {3,6,9,12}
};
```

Figure 7.4 Two-dimensional array memory allocation with values

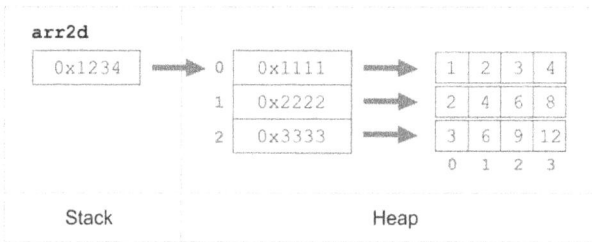

Take a look at this example:

```
1    // MultiplicationTable.java
2    public class MultiplicationTable {
3        public static void main(String[] args) {
4            int[][] arr2d = new int [3][4];
5
6            for (int i = 0; i < arr2d.length; i++) {
7                for (int j = 0; j < arr2d[i].length; j++) {
8                    arr2d[i][j] = (i + 1) * (j + 1);
9                    System.out.print(arr2d[i][j] + "\t");
10               }
11               System.out.println();
12           }
13       }
14   }
```

This is a sample of the multiplication table having 3 rows and 4 columns. As you notice, all the data types in their columns and rows are of the same type. Here is its output once you compile and run this:

```
1    2    3    4
2    4    6    8
3    6    9    12
```

7.6.2 Non-Rectangular Arrays

Since you are allowed to declare an array of arrays, you can also create a non-rectangular array of arrays. This means you can declare arrays this way.

```
int[][] irregularArray = new int [4][];

irregularArray[0] = new int [3];     // 1
irregularArray[1] = new int [5];     // 2
irregularArray[2] = new int [1];     // 3
irregularArray[3] = new int [4];     // 4
```

As you notice, array `irregularArray[0]` can only hold 3 integer values, while array `irregularArray[1]` can hold up to 5 integer values. Even though it is a non-rectangular array, its respective default values will still be assigned upon creation.

Figure 7.5 **A non-rectangular array with default values**

Here are the commonly encountered errors in declaring a non-rectangular array:

Incorrect Syntax Example:

```
int[][] jaggedArray = new int[3][];
jaggedArray = {
        {10, 20},
        {30, 40, 50},
        {60}
};
```

This code results in a compile-time error because you cannot directly assign a block of values ({ . . . }) to an already initialized array reference without using the new keyword properly.

Corrected Version:

```
int[][] jaggedArray = {
        {1, 2},
        {3, 4, 5},
        {6}
};
```

Or if you want to do it step-by-step:

```
int[][] jaggedArray = new int[3][];
jaggedArray[0] = new int[]{1, 2};
jaggedArray[1] = new int[]{3, 4, 5};
jaggedArray[2] = new int[]{6};
```

In Java, arrays represent one of the most essential and straightforward data structures to store fixed-size collections of elements of the same data type. When an array is created, its elements are automatically initialized with default values based on the type. The size of an array can be determined using the `.length` attribute, which is useful for controlling loop execution and avoiding index errors. Java provides multiple techniques for working with arrays efficiently. The enhanced for loop offers a cleaner and more readable approach to iterating through array elements. Additionally, the `System.arraycopy()` method simplifies the task of copying data between arrays.

Java also allows the use of command-line arguments, which are passed as an array of strings to the `main` method, providing an alternative way to receive input.

Furthermore, Java supports both one-dimensional and two-dimensional arrays. Two-dimensional arrays are implemented as arrays of single-dimensional arrays, allowing for the creation of rectangular and non-rectangular (jagged) array structures.

Chapter Summary

- Arrays are the simplest data structure in most programming languages, including Java.

- Arrays have initial values upon creation.

- Array limits can be determined using the .length attribute.

- The enhanced for-loop can be an alternative way to iterate through an array.

- The System.arraycopy() method is the easiest way to copy the contents of an array.

- Command-line arguments are an alternative way to accept string values in Java.

- Two-dimensional arrays are treated as an array of single-dimensional arrays.

- Both rectangular and non-rectangular arrays are features in Java.

Quiz

1. **Which of the following statements about arrays in Java is NOT TRUE?**

   a. Arrays in Java will have a size once it is created. You can know the size of the array by calling the `.length` attribute

   b. The elements in an array are accessed using a non-negative integer index.

   c. The elements of the array are referenced using integer indexes from 0 to n-1, inclusive.

   d. To get the number of elements of an array, we can use the method `size()`.

2. **If I have an array having 10 elements, what is the legal range of index values?**

   a. 1 to 10

   b. 0 to 9

   c. 0 to 10

   d. The index depends on the data type of the arrays

3. **Given the array declaration:**

```
int[] myArray = {10, 20, 30, 40, 50};
```

   Choose the correct way to get the size of the array.

   a. `myArray[].length`

   b. `myArray.size`

   c. `myArray[].size`

   d. `myArray.length`

4. Given the code snippet:

```
int sum = 0;
int[] myArray = {10, 20, 30, 40, 50};
```

Which enhanced for loop should we use in order to compute the sum of all the elements in the array?

a. `for (int n : myArray) sum =+ n;`

b. `for (myArray : n) sum += n;`

c. `for (int n : myArray) sum += n;`

d. `for (int n : myArray[]) sum += n;`

5. Given the code body of the class MyCode:

```
public class MyCode {
    public static void main(String[] args) {
        System.out.println(args[0] + args[1] + args[2]);
    }
}
```

Given the CommandLine argument call:

```
java MyCode 10 20 30
```

What will be the output?

a. 102030

b. 60

c. 10 20 30

d. `ArrayIndexOutOfBoundsException` will occur at runtime.

6. Consider the following sample code snippet:

```
public static void main(String[] args) {
    System.out.print(args[0]);
    System.out.print(args[1]);
    System.out.print(args[2]);
}
```

Given the command line arguments, executing the file MyJavaCode:

```
java MyJavaCode apple "bike bike" cat <ENTER>
```

What will be the output during runtime?

a. An error will occur during runtime.
b. applebikecat
c. applebikebike
d. applebike bikecat

7. If I have an array having 100 elements, what is the legal range of index values?

a. 0 to 99
b. 1 to 99
c. 1 to 100
d. The values depend on the operating systems.

8. Given the following array declaration, which one is the INCORRECT way to declare an array?

a. char ch[][] = new char[2][3];
b. int[] a[] = new int[][2];
c. boolean [] bool [] = new boolean[1][];
d. byte[][] b = new byte[10][20];

9. **Given the declaration:**

```
int[][] jaggedArr = {{1, 2}, {3, 4, 5}, {6, 7, 8, 9}};
```

Which of the following options will print the size of the shortest array?

a. `System.out.println(jaggedArr[2].length);`
b. `System.out.println(jaggedArr[1].length);`
c. `System.out.println(jaggedArr[0].length);`
d. `System.out.println(jaggedArr[3].length);`

10. **Given the following code, what will be the output?**

```
public class ArrayTest {
    public static void main(String[] args) {
        int[] arr = {1, 2, 3, 4, 5};
        int sum = 0;
        for (int i = 0; i < arr.length; i++) {
            sum += arr[i] * (i % 2 == 0 ? 1 : -1);
        }
        System.out.println(sum);
    }
}
```

a. 3
b. 1
c. 5
d. 7

Answers				
1 – d	2 – b	3 – d	4 – c	5 – a
6 – d	7 – a	8 – b	9 – c	10 – a

Coding Task

Coding Task 1:

Create a Java program that will ask the user to input any type of String values via a command line. The output should contain the args[i] value, the length of the input String, the actual String, and the type of character of the last character of the input String. The types of characters are as follows: vowels, consonants, numbers, and symbols. The only time you can consider a certain character as a symbol is when it is not a vowel, nor a consonant, nor a number.

Here's a sample IO:

```
java ArrayExercise productiveWork 7654321 javajava $$$ <ENTER>
```

Output:

```
args[0] = productiveWork = 14 = consonant
args[1] = 7654321 = 7 = number
args[2] = javajava = 8 = vowel
args[3] = $$$ = 3 = symbol
```

Coding Task 2:

Write a Java program that accepts two positive integer values from the command line. The first value represents the number of rows. The second value represents the number of columns.

Use these two values to generate and display a multiplication table, where each cell contains the product of its corresponding row and column numbers.

Here's a sample IO:

```
java MultiplicationTable 3 5 <ENTER>
```

Output:

```
Multiplication Table (3 rows x 5 columns)
1   2   3   4    5
2   4   6   8    10
3   6   9   12   15
```

Coding Task 3:

Write a Java program that takes an array of strings via the command line (e.g., names of fruits), and prints the elements in reverse order.

Here's a sample IO:

```
java ReverseArrayElements Apple Banana Cherry <ENTER>
```

Use a for loop that starts from the last index down to the first. Print each element on a new line.

Output:

```
Original order: Apple, Banana, Cherry
Reversed order:
Cherry
Banana
Apple
```

Coding Task 4:

Create a Java program that will accept 5 integer values and store them in an array of int. The program should identify and print the largest value in the array.

Here's a sample IO:

```
Enter 5 integer values:
75 <ENTER>
-3 <ENTER>
50 <ENTER>
98 <ENTER>
1 <ENTER>
```

Output:

```
The highest number in the array is: 98
```

Practice More, Get Better!

Additional coding tasks for this chapter are available in the exclusive online resources that accompany this book.

Glossary

Array: A container object that holds a fixed number of values of a single type.

Array Limits: The fixed size of an array once it is created; cannot be changed.

Array of Arrays (Two-dimensional Arrays): Arrays where each element is itself an array; used to represent matrices or tables.

Block: A group of zero or more statements enclosed in braces { }.

Break Statement: Used to exit a loop or `switch` statement prematurely.

Coding Conventions: A set of guidelines for writing code to improve readability and maintainability.

Command Line Arguments: Parameters passed to the `main()` method when a Java program is executed from the terminal.

Compile-Time Errors: Errors detected by the compiler due to incorrect syntax or misuse of Java language rules.

Continue Statement: Skips the current iteration of a loop and proceeds to the next cycle.

Debugging: The process of identifying and fixing bugs in code.

do-while Loop: A control flow statement that executes a block of code at least once, and then repeatedly based on a condition.

Enhanced `for` loop: A simplified loop used to iterate through arrays or collections without an index variable.

for Loop: A control flow statement for executing a block of code a fixed number of times.

Garbage Collector: An automatic memory management process that reclaims memory occupied by objects no longer in use.

HelloWorld: The traditional first program that outputs `Hello, World!` to demonstrate basic syntax.

Identifiers: Names used to identify variables, methods, classes, and other user-defined elements.

`if` Condition: A control structure that executes a block of code if a specified condition is true.

Java: A high-level, class-based, object-oriented programming language known for its portability and security.

Java Development Kit (JDK): A software development kit used to develop Java applications, including the JRE, compiler, and tools.

Java Keywords: Reserved words in Java that have a predefined meaning in the language syntax.

Java Operators: Symbols that perform operations on variables and values (e.g., +, −, *, /).

Java Technology Flavors: Variants of Java platforms such as Java SE, Java EE, and Java ME.

JSHELL: A command-line tool introduced in Java 9 for quickly running Java code snippets interactively.

JRE (Java Runtime Environment): A part of the JDK that enables Java applications to run, but does not include development tools.

Labelled `breaks` / `continues`: Special forms of `break` / `continue` that affect outer loops when nested loops are used.

Linux JDK Installer: The process or software used to install the JDK on Linux operating systems.

Math Class: A Java utility class providing mathematical functions such as trigonometry, rounding, and exponentiation.

Mac OS X JDK Installer: The process or software used to install the JDK on macOS systems.

Non-Rectangular Arrays: Also called jagged arrays; two-dimensional arrays with rows of varying lengths.

Order of Precedence: Rules that determine the sequence in which operators are evaluated in expressions.

Primitive Data Types: Basic data types in Java, such as `int`, `char`, `boolean`, `double`, etc.

Runtime Errors: Errors that occur during the execution of a program, such as division by zero.

S`canner` Class: A class used to obtain user input in Java from various input sources, including the keyboard.

Semicolons: Symbols used to terminate statements in Java.

`String` **Class:** Represents sequences of characters and is widely used for text processing.

`String` **Methods:** Built-in functions for manipulating and analyzing strings.

`StringBuffer` **Class:** A mutable sequence of characters that is thread-safe.

`StringBuilder` **Class:** Similar to `StringBuffer` but not synchronized, offering better performance in single-threaded contexts.

`switch-case` **Statement:** A control structure that executes one block of code from multiple options based on a variable's value.

`System.out.println()`: A method used to print output to the console, followed by a new line.

Two-dimensional Arrays: See Array of Arrays.

User Input: Data provided by the user at runtime, commonly collected using the `Scanner` class.

Variables: Containers for storing data values.

White Spaces: Non-visible characters (spaces, tabs, line breaks) that help separate tokens in code but are ignored by the compiler.

while Loop: A control structure that repeats a block of code as long as a condition remains true.

Windows JDK Installer: The process or software used to install the JDK on Windows operating systems.

NOTES

www.ingramcontent.com/pod-product-compliance
Lightning Source LLC
Chambersburg PA
CBHW060239220326
41598CB00027B/3986